Also from FranklinCovey

The 7 Habits of Highly Effective People

The 7 Habits of Highly Effective People Journal

The 7 Habits of Highly Effective Families

Living the 7 Habits

Principle-Centered Leadership

First Things First

The 7 Habits of Highly Effective Teens

The 7 Habits of Highly Effective Teens Journal

Life Matters

What Matters Most

The 10 Natural Laws of Successful Time and Life Management

businessThink

The Power Principle

Breakthrough Factor

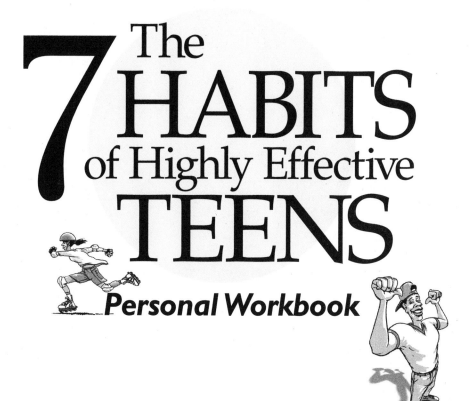

The 7 HABITS of Highly Effective TEENS

Personal Workbook

Sean Covey

A FIRESIDE BOOK
Published by Simon & Schuster
New York   London   Toronto   Sydney

FIRESIDE
Rockefeller Center
1230 Avenue of the Americas
New York, NY 10020

For information on how to become a licensed FranklinCovey trainer,
call 1-800-272-6839.

For information regarding special discounts for bulk purchases,
please contact Simon & Schuster Special Sales at
1-800-456-6798 or business@simonandschuster.com.

Designed by Ruth Lee

20

Library of Congress Cataloging-in-Publication Data is available.

ISBN-13: 978-0-7432-5098-6 (Pbk)
ISBN-10:   0-7432-5098-2 (Pbk)

Contents

Welcome!

You may be thinking, "How did I end up with this workbook in my hands? Don't I already have enough work from school?"

I don't blame you for thinking that. I felt the same way when I was a teen. Let me introduce myself. My name is Sean and I wrote this workbook, which is a companion workbook to the book *The 7 Habits of Highly Effective Teens*. You see, although I am a retired teenager, I still remember what it was like to be one. I could have sworn I was riding an emotional roller coaster back then. As I look back, I can't believe I survived. Barely. And yet, after all I went through, I have to admit that life is even tougher for today's teens. It's no longer a playground. It's a jungle out there. I recently talked with a bunch of teens and asked them, "What are your biggest challenges?" This is what they said:

"Doing well in school."
"Getting along with my parents."
"Feeling good about myself."
"Fitting in and making friends."
"Dealing with dating and sex."
"Making good choices about drinking, smoking, and doing drugs."

There were lots of other challenges mentioned, but these seemed to be the big ones. And that is why I wrote *The 7 Habits of Highly Effective Teens* book and this workbook. I wrote it to help you deal with these challenges and get through the jungle—not just barely alive but better and stronger.

This workbook was designed with you in mind. It is packed full of fun activities, personal quizzes, introspective questions, and much more. But don't worry, it won't feel like schoolwork. It is more like a personal journal, designed to help you think deeply about your life and explore your own strengths and weaknesses. (So, if you don't want anyone else to read it, don't let them.) It will help you see clearly where you are headed in life. It will challenge you. It will help you identify where you may have gone astray, and it will help you renew yourself. It will ask you to record some of your innermost feelings and desires. All in all, it will help you build better habits for a happier life.

How to Get the Most from This Workbook

As you make your way through this workbook, here are a few tips that will make it a great experience:

- Mark it up! Don't be afraid to get out your colored pencils or markers and highlight the stuff you want to remember. Scribble in the margins. Doodle. Make notes to yourself. Books and workbooks are meant to be written in. So make it your own. Have fun with it!
- Write, write, write. Give the activities and exercises a try. The more you write, the more about yourself will come out. You may be surprised to discover entirely new aspects of yourself that you never knew existed.
- Find your favorite quotes. The workbook has a ton of really cool quotes. So find the ones you like, write them down, and post them where you can see them, like on a mirror or in your locker.
- Apply the 7 Habits to "your" life. Don't do the workbook thing: "If only my friend had this workbook," or "Wow! Could my parents use this stuff!" Instead, focus on how you can improve "you" and apply this information to your own challenges.
- Share what you learn. Discuss your favorite ideas with a close friend or your mom or your dad or guardian or some other adult who is special to you. Tell them about the commitments you've made and how you want to change and ask for their help.
- Jump around. You don't have to go through the workbook from front to back. Skip around and do the activities you feel like doing at any given time. It will be more fun this way.

USE *THE 7 HABITS OF HIGHLY EFFECTIVE TEENS* BOOK

To get the most from this workbook, you're better off having a copy of *The 7 Habits of Highly Effective Teens* book to use as a companion piece. The book will provide you with the background and explanations of the 7 Habits and has some great stories so that everything will make sense. In the workbook, I'll give you the page numbers so that you can quickly refer back to the book when you need a refresher.

THINK ABOUT WHAT YOU WANT TO LEARN

Finally, take a few minutes now and glance through the workbook to begin to get an idea of what this workbook concept is all about. Now, write down your personal expectations, based on the following major points:

After I finish this workbook, I hope to have learned:

The biggest challenge I am facing now is:

This workbook can help me deal with that challenge by:

I hope you enjoy your personal journey through this workbook. Happy trails!

Get in the **H**abit

What Exactly Are Habits?  **R**ead pages 5–6 of the *Teens* book. The 7 Habits of Highly Effective Teens are:

Habit 1: **Be Proactive—**
Take responsibility for your life.

Habit 2: **Begin with the End in Mind—**
Define your mission and goals in life.

Habit 3: **Put First Things First—**
Prioritize, and do the most important things first.

Habit 4: **Think Win-Win—**
Have an everyone-can-win attitude.

Habit 5: **Seek First to Understand, Then to Be Understood—**
Listen to people sincerely.

Habit 6: **Synergize—**
Work together to achieve more.

Habit 7: **Sharpen the Saw—**
Renew yourself regularly.

> We first make our habits, and then our habits make us.
>
> —JOHN DRYDEN

Habits are things you do repeatedly. But most of the time you are hardly aware you do them. They're on autopilot. Depending on what they are, your habits will either make

I

you or break you. You become what you repeatedly do. Luckily, you are stronger than your habits.

Let's look at some of the good habits you have in your life right now. (Good habits include things such as exercising regularly, being a loyal friend, or being on time.)

Think About Your Habits

Four of my really great habits are:

1. _____
2. _____
3. _____
4. _____

The reason I keep these habits in my life is:

The good results I get from having each good habit are: (For example: I have a habit of smiling at people I meet, and now people are friendlier to me.)

Habits aren't always positive. In fact, they can be good, bad, or just neutral. Some habits I have that are neutral (they're neither good nor bad—they're just habits) are: (For example: I put on one sock and then a shoe, then the other sock and the other shoe.)

Now let's list some habits you're not so proud of. Complete the statements that follow:

Right now, my worst habits are:

The reason I have these bad habits is:

I've had these bad habits for (days, weeks, years?):

The bad results I get from having these bad habits are: (For example: I am late to school, which means I miss class discussion and get demerits toward my citizenship grade.)

From my list of bad habits above, the one habit I would like to change the most is:

Change the Bad to Good

On the table below, fill in the habits that you named above. Keep this table handy during the upcoming week and use it as a tool to help you remember to change your bad habits to good ones.

BAD HABIT I WANT TO CHANGE	GOOD HABIT I WANT TO REPLACE IT WITH

In School:

1. _____   1. _____

2. _____   2. _____

3. _____   3. _____

With My Family:

1. _____   1. _____

2. _____   2. _____

3. _____   3. _____

With My Friends:

1. _____   1. _____

2 _____   2. _____

3._____   3. _____

Other:

1. _____   1. _____

2._____   2. _____

3._____   3. _____

A cool thing about the 7 Habits is how they build on each other. It's a progression—just like learning arithmetic before calculus, learning the alphabet before learning to spell, or building a solid foundation before building a 150-story building. Trees grow this way, too; they put down solid roots before the trunk, branches, or leaves begin to grow.

Fill in the habits on the tree that follows from what you have learned so far.

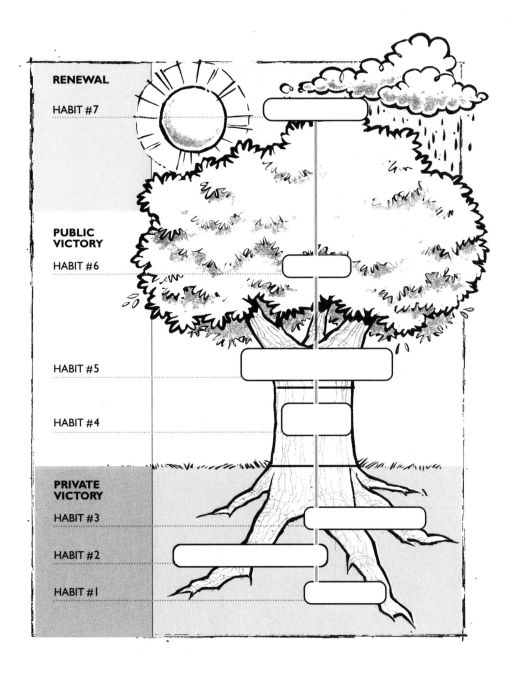

RENEWAL

HABIT #7

PUBLIC
VICTORY

HABIT #6

HABIT #5

HABIT #4

PRIVATE
VICTORY

HABIT #3

HABIT #2

HABIT #1

Paradigms and Principles

WHAT YOU SEE IS WHAT YOU GET

So What's a Paradigm? A paradigm is the way you see something—your point of view, frame of reference, or belief. As you may have noticed, sometimes your paradigms can be accurate, way off the mark, wrong, or incomplete.

Did you know that from medieval times until the late 1800s doctors believed that a sick person had diseased blood? Doctors would "bleed" a person of the blood until they believed that they had drained the "diseased blood." This is, in fact, what killed George Washington, not the sore throat and fever he was suffering from.

We now know about germs and that they can be in different parts of the body and in different forms. So now we treat illnesses with a different form of healing—we no longer "bleed" a patient. That was an inaccurate and an incomplete way of looking at healing.

> Paradigms are like glasses. When you have incomplete paradigms about yourself or life in general, it's like wearing glasses with the wrong prescription. Those lenses affect how you see everything else.
>
> —SEAN COVEY

Top 10 All-Time Stupid Quotes:

10 "There is no reason for any individual to have a computer in their home."

KENNETH OLSEN, PRESIDENT AND FOUNDER OF DIGITAL EQUIPMENT CORPORATION, IN 1977

9 "Airplanes are interesting toys but of no military value."
MARSHAL FERDINAND FOCH, FRENCH MILITARY STRATEGIST AND
FUTURE WORLD WAR I COMMANDER, IN 1911

8 "[Man will never reach the moon] regardless of all future scientific advances."
DR. LEE DE FOREST, INVENTOR OF THE AUDION TUBE AND FATHER OF RADIO,
ON FEBRUARY 25, 1967

7 "[Television] won't be able to hold on to any market it captures after the first six months. People will soon get tired of staring at a plywood box every night."
DARRYL F. ZANUCK, HEAD OF 20TH CENTURY FOX, IN 1946

6 "We don't like their sound. Groups of guitars are on the way out."
DECCA RECORDS REJECTING THE BEATLES, IN 1962

5 "For the majority of people, the use of tobacco has a beneficial effect."
DR. IAN G. MACDONALD, LOS ANGELES SURGEON,
AS QUOTED IN *NEWSWEEK*, NOVEMBER 18, 1969

4 "This 'telephone' has too many shortcomings to be seriously considered as a means of communication. The device is inherently of no value to us."
WESTERN UNION INTERNAL MEMO, IN 1876

3 "The earth is the center of the universe."
PTOLEMY, THE GREAT EGYPTIAN ASTRONOMER, IN THE SECOND CENTURY

2 "Nothing of importance happened today."
WRITTEN BY KING GEORGE III OF ENGLAND ON JULY 4, 1776

 "Everything that can be invented has been invented."
CHARLES H. DUELL, U.S. COMMISSIONER OF PATENTS, IN 1899

What are some other paradigms from history that have proved to be inaccurate or incomplete? (For example: The world is flat.)

What kind of impact did these inaccurate paradigms from history have on the world?

● PARADIGMS OF SELF

A paradigm is the way you see something—your point of view, frame of reference, or belief. So a paradigm of self is how you see yourself.

No matter how you see yourself, you're probably right. If you think you are good at school, then you can be good at school. If you think you are no good at math, then you'll be no good at math. Paradigms of self can help or hinder you. Positive self-paradigms can bring out the best in you, while negative self-paradigms can limit you.

Some positive paradigms I have about myself are:

If someone were going to name something after me, it would be:

Some negative paradigms I have about myself are:

Paradigms that my parents or guardians, boss at work, or teachers at school might have about me are:

Their paradigms match mine (true or false):

Could they be right? How will I find out?

Self-Paradigm Assessment

Read the Paradigms of Self section on pages 13–16 of the *Teens* book. Now, evaluate how you see yourself by completing the assessment below.

	YES	NO
I am someone who cares about others' feelings.		
I am good at school.		
I am a kind person.		
I am generally a happy person.		
I am intelligent.		
I am helpful.		
I am a good athlete.		
I am talented.		
I am a go-getter.		
I am a good member of my family.		
I am a bad person.		
I am lazy.		
I am rarely happy.		
I am not smart.		
I am not good at anything.		
I am not attractive.		

	YES	NO
I am not popular.		
I am not a good friend.		
I am not honest.		
I am not reliable.		

If you identified at least one negative self-paradigm during the assessment, complete the statement below:

One negative paradigm I would like to change is:

Paradigm Builder

If your self-paradigms are all wrong, what do you do?

Spend time with someone who believes in me and recognizes my potential. For me, this person is:

SOMEDAY...

Drop friends who tear me down or believe I am like them. Friends I may need to drop are:

Try to see things from other people's points of view to shift the paradigm. A situation I need to see the other side of is:

● PARADIGMS OF OTHERS

In the Paradigms and Principles chapter you learn that you have paradigms not only about yourself but also about other people. And they can be way out of whack. Seeing things from a different point of view can help you understand why other people act the way they do. Sometimes you judge people without having all the facts.

> Friendship with one's self is all important, because without it one cannot be friends with anyone else in the world.
>
> —ELEANOR ROOSEVELT

Your paradigms are often incomplete, inaccurate, or completely messed up. Therefore, you shouldn't be quick to judge, label, or form rigid opinions of others, or of yourself, for that matter. From your limited point of view, you seldom see the whole picture, or have all the facts. You should open your mind and heart to new information, ideas, and points of view, and be willing to change your paradigms when it becomes clear that they're wrong.

Someone I may have judged inaccurately without having all the details is:

I will change that paradigm by: (Describe the actions you can take immediately.)

FRANK & ERNEST by Bob Thaves

I can help others understand that their paradigms might be incomplete by: (Describe your actions or plan.)

• PARADIGMS OF LIFE

Besides having paradigms about yourself and others, you have paradigms about the world in general. Whatever is important to you will become your paradigm, your glasses, or your life center. For teens, popular life centers include friends, stuff, boyfriends/girlfriends, school, parents, sports or hobbies, heroes, enemies, self, and work. Each of these life centers has its good points, but they are all incomplete in one way or another. The Paradigms and Principles chapter explains that you can always count on one center—principles.

If you don't take control of your life, don't complain when others do.

—BETH MENDE CONNY

To help determine your life center, answer the following survey.

A B C D E F

1. You are at home on a Tuesday night doing your trigonometry homework. It's slow-going and boring. You hear your friends drive up to the curb and yell that they're heading out to dinner. What do you do?
   a. If you decide to keep doing your homework, even though it's boring, put a checkmark in box F.
   b. If you decide to go with your friends and tell yourself that you can always do your homework later, put a checkmark in box A.

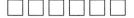

2. Your family is planning a five-day summer vacation to Florida. You want to go, but taking five days off work means that you won't earn as much to buy clothes for school. What do you do?
   a. If you decide to stay home and continue working, put a checkmark in box B.
   b. If you decide to go with your family to Florida, put a checkmark in box F.

3. You are at home getting ready to go out with your friends—they'll be there any minute. The phone rings and it's your boyfriend/girlfriend. He's/She's wondering if you can come over right now to hang out and watch a video. What do you do?
   a. If you decide to go to your boyfriend's/girlfriend's house, put a checkmark in box C.
   b. If you decide to tell your boyfriend/girlfriend that you have plans with your friends, put a checkmark in box F.

4. It's 11:00 P.M. and you're studying for your English lit test. You've been studying all evening and you're pretty sure you'll do well on the test tomorrow. You're tired and want to go to bed. But you have an A– average in the class, and if you study a little longer to ensure that you ace the test, you can bring your average up to a solid A. What do you do?
   a. If you decide to go to bed to renew yourself, put a checkmark in box F.
   b. If you decide to stay up longer to ace the test, put a checkmark in box D.

A   B   C   D   E   F

5. You're attending college recruitment day at your school and are sitting in one of the presentations. You're overwhelmed. You have no idea what you want to be "when you grow up," and you have no idea which college to attend. The presentation you're in is for the college your mother wants you to go to. You don't know what you want to do, but you'd rather just have the decision over with. At the end of the presentation the presenter asks the class to fill out applications. What do you do?
   a. If you decide to wait and fill out an application after you've thought about your options a little more, put a checkmark in box F.
   b. If you decide to fill out an application, put a checkmark in box E.

Count up the number of checkmarks in each column and record the numbers here: A: _____ B: _____ C: _____ D: _____ E: _____ F: _____

Answer key:

Box F: If you have a 3 or higher in this column, you have a pretty healthy life center.

Box E: If you have a 1 in this column, read page 22 of the *Teens* book to examine if your life is too parent-centered.

Box D: If you have a 1 in this column, read page 21 of the *Teens* book. School is important, but don't overdo it! You also might want to pay special attention when we talk about renewal in Habit 7.

Box C: If you have a 1 in this column, read page 20 of the *Teens* book to examine if your life is too boyfriend/girlfriend-centered.

Box B: If you have a 1 in this column, read page 19 of the *Teens* book. There is nothing wrong with accomplishing and enjoying your stuff, but never center your life on things that in the end have no lasting value. Great memories of vacations and family times will last forever.

Box A: If you have a 1 in this column, read page 19 of the *Teens* book to examine if your life is too friend-centered.

PRINCIPLES NEVER FAIL

We are all familiar with the effects of gravity. Throw a ball up and it comes down. It's a natural law or principle. Just as there are principles that rule the physical world, there are principles that rule the human world. If you live by them, you will excel. If you break them, you will fail.

Principles include things like honesty, service, love, hard work, respect, gratitude, moderation, fairness, integrity, loyalty, and responsibility. The Paradigms and Principles chapter teaches that just as a compass always points to true north, your heart will recognize true principles. A principle-centered life is simply the most stable, immovable, and unshakable foundation you can build on.

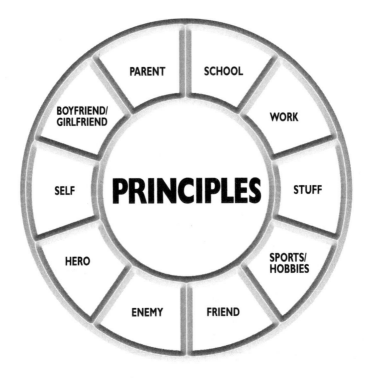

To fully understand why you should live a life based on principles, just imagine living a life based on the opposite—a life of dishonesty, laziness, ingratitude, selfishness, and hate. Putting principles first is the key to doing better in all you do. For instance, if you live the principles of service, respect, and love, you're likely to have more good, solid friends and more stable relationships.

Some other principles I can think of are:

Of the principles I listed, the most difficult for me to live is:

Think of principles as your life center and your hobbies and interests as spokes on the wheel. In the center of the wheel below, fill in a principle that you live by now or admire in others. On the spokes, list the things that the principle influences (hobbies, school, work, etc.).

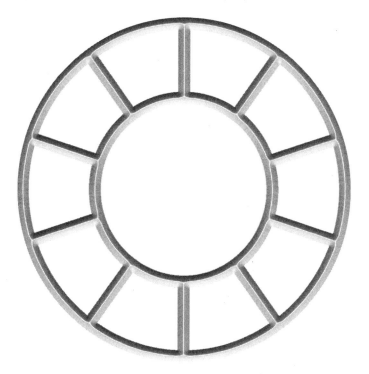

Some principles I would like to cultivate are:

I will cultivate them by: (Describe your actions or plan.)

The date that I will begin doing this is:

Decide today to make principles your life center or paradigm. Whenever you face a dilemma or difficult situation, ask yourself, "What is the principle in play here?"

Baby Steps are small, easy exercises you can do now to help you apply the principle or habit to your life. These small, easy steps can help you achieve your larger and long-term goals. At the end of every chapter in the *Teens* book, and at the end of every section in this workbook, you will find a list of Baby Steps. Be daring and do one or two.

 The next time you look in the mirror, say something positive about yourself.

 Show appreciation for someone's point of view today. Say something like, "Hey, that is a cool idea."

3. Think of a limiting paradigm you might have of yourself, such as "I'm not outgoing." Now, do something today that totally contradicts that paradigm.

4. Think of a loved one or close friend who has been acting out of character lately. Consider what might be causing him or her to act that way.

 When you have nothing to do, what is it that occupies your thoughts? Remember, whatever is most important to you will become your paradigm or life-center.

What occupies my time and energy? _____

_____

6. The Golden Rule rules! Begin today to treat others as you would want them to treat you. Don't be impatient, complain about leftovers, or bad-mouth someone, unless you want the same treatment.

7. Sometime soon, find a quiet place where you can be alone. Think about what matters most to you.

8. Listen carefully to the lyrics of the music you listen to most frequently. Evaluate if they are in harmony with the principles you believe in.

9. When you do your chores at home or work tonight, try out the principle of hard work. Go the extra mile and do more than is expected.

10. The next time you're in a tough situation and don't know what to do, ask yourself, "What principle should I apply (e.g., honesty, love, loyalty, hard work, patience)?" Now, follow the principle and don't look back.

Which of the Baby Steps did I try, and what did I learn?

The **Personal Bank Account**

STARTING WITH THE MAN IN THE MIRROR

Inside Out **I**n the Personal Bank Account (PBA) chapter, you learn that all change begins with "the man in the mirror." In fact, some of the hardest battles in life are the ones fought within yourself. Through these battles, you learn to tap into your inner strength and develop character— then you truly grow.

KA-CHING!

If you want to change the world, begin with yourself, not with your parents, your boyfriend or girlfriend, or your teacher. All change begins with you. It's inside out. Not outside in.

Read the writings of the Anglican bishop on page 33 of the *Teens* book, then complete the statements below:

> I'm starting with the man in the mirror
> I'm asking him to change his ways
> And no message could have been any clearer
> If you wanna make the world a better place
> Take a look at yourself, and then make a change.
>
> —"MAN IN THE MIRROR"
> BY SIEDAH GARRETT
> AND GLEN BALLARD

If I could change something about the world, it would be:

One change I could make in myself that might help bring about that worldwide change is:

I think that an inside-out change could help others around me because:

> The real tragedy is the tragedy of the man who never in his life braces himself for his one supreme effort— he never stretches to his full capacity, never stands up to his full stature.
>
> —ARNOLD BENNETT

THE PERSONAL BANK ACCOUNT (PBA)

How you feel about yourself is like a bank account. Just like a checking or savings account at a bank, you can make deposits into or withdrawals from your PBA by the things you think, say, and do. For example, when you stick to a commitment you've made to yourself, you feel in control. It's a deposit. On the other hand, when you break a promise to yourself, you feel disappointed and make a withdrawal.

To keep a positive balance in the account, you need to have more deposits than withdrawals. The more deposits you make into your PBA, the better you feel about yourself. If you make too many withdrawals, your self-esteem and confidence will drop.

How Is Your PBA?

How much trust and confidence do you have in yourself? Do you have a positive or negative PBA? Review these possible symptoms to see if the balance in your PBA is pretty dismal:

- You don't stand up for yourself when you know you're in the right.

- You make degrading comments about yourself.

- You always go along with what the crowd is doing or saying.

- You overindulge in food, TV watching, or Web surfing.

- You use drugs or alcohol.

- You aren't loyal to anyone or anything.

- You allow others to use you.

A positive PBA includes these symptoms:

+ You speak up when you know you're right.

+ You have the self-confidence to let others know of your opinions and good ideas.

+ You are happy for others' success.

+ You have a good balance of school, physical activities, working on talents, and personal time.

+ You live by principles.

+ If someone speaks ill of someone you know and care about, you have the courage to defend that person.

+ You work to improve and build your skills and talents.

+ You recognize life's natural ups and downs.

To get a clear picture of your Personal Bank Account, keep track of the deposits and withdrawals you make during one week. Carry a PBA checkbook register (as shown at right) with you for seven days. Record your actions in the register and assign a deposit or withdrawal value to each. For example, each deposit you make is worth $1 to $100; however, withdrawals cost from $50 to $200. You get to determine how much to add or subtract. See how many deposits you can make to yourself in a week. Be totally honest with yourself about your withdrawals.

Personal Bank Account

	+	−
Started the exercise program I promised myself I'd start	50	
Stayed up late last night		150
Prepared for big chemistry exam coming up in a few days	100	
Told myself how great I look	20	
Came home from school and chatted online for hours		120
Skipped breakfast, had a candy bar and soda pop for lunch		50
Balance		

After a week, are you pleased with the results? Or are you surprised at how many withdrawals you made?

KEEP PROMISES TO YOURSELF

Have you ever had friends or roommates who seldom came through? They say they'll call you and they don't. They promise to pick you up for the game and they forget. After a while, you don't trust them. Their commitments mean squat. The same thing occurs when you continually make and break self-promises, such as, "I'm going to get up at 6 A.M. tomorrow morning," or "I'm going to get my homework done right when I get home." After a while, you don't trust yourself.

You should treat the commitments you make to yourself as seriously as those you make to the most important people in your life. If you're feeling out of control in your life, focus on the single thing you can control—yourself. Make a promise to yourself and keep it.

Start Small and Build

Keeping big commitments to yourself is easier if you make small ones you know you can keep; then go bigger—to the more difficult promises.

Complete the statements below:

When I promise myself I will do something but don't keep the promise, I feel:

> I believe life is constantly testing us for our level of commitment, and life's greatest rewards are reserved for those who demonstrate a never-ending commitment to act until they achieve.
>
> —ANTHONY ROBBINS

The promise to myself I wish I could keep, but keep failing to do, is:

The reason I can't keep this promise is:

The two or three little promises to myself that, if done, would help me keep the big promise are:

1. _____
2. _____
3. _____

I want to keep the big promise because:

My life would be better because:

The great thing I could give myself as a reward for keeping the big promise is:

Do Small Acts of Kindness

Doing small acts of kindness is an extraordinary way to help you feel better about yourself. Even though the kind acts are for someone else, they add up to major deposits in your PBA.

Doing small acts of kindness gets you focused outward instead of inward. It's hard to be depressed

while serving someone else, so as a result of helping others, you end up feeling wonderful yourself.

Read the Do Small Acts of Kindness section on pages 35–37 of the *Teens* book. Complete the statements and read the story below:

Three people in my life who could benefit from an act of kindness are:

1. _____

2. _____

3. _____

Read the following story:

"Why does it always take so long to get through this tollbooth?" Jayden thought to himself as he sat in a long line of cars waiting for his turn to pay the toll and get back on the road. The cars inched forward— little by little. Jayden drummed his fingers nervously on the steering wheel and pushed his hand through his hair. "Great," he thought. "Now I'm really going to be late to pick up the guys. We'll never make it to the game before tip-off." Five more minutes passed and Jayden's patience was gone. Suddenly, the line of cars in front of him quickly disappeared—five cars drove through the tollbooth in little time. Jayden couldn't believe his luck! Suddenly he was at the tollbooth. As he pulled up, the attendant said to him, "No need to pay. A car six cars ahead of you paid the toll for the next ten cars." Jayden smiled and pulled out onto the road.

How do you think Jayden felt during the rest of his drive to the game? How do you think the anonymous toll-paying driver felt?

Someone who did an anonymous act of kindness toward me was:

The act of kindness he or she performed was:

That act of kindness made me feel:

An anonymous act of kindness I could do for the three people I listed on page 26 is:

1. _____

2. _____

3. _____

BE GENTLE WITH YOURSELF

In the Personal Bank Account (PBA) chapter, you learn that no one is perfect, so you shouldn't be too hard on yourself when you make mistakes. Being gentle means admitting to yourself that you will probably mess up every day and then forgiving yourself when you do. It means not expecting to be perfect by tomorrow morning. It means learning to laugh at the stupid things you do.

> In nature, nothing is perfect and everything is perfect. Trees can be contorted, bent in weird ways, and they're still beautiful.
>
> —ALICE WALKER

Learn from your mistakes—don't beat yourself up over them. The past is just that—the past. Recognize what went wrong and why. Make amends if you need to. Then drop it and move on.

Laugh at Yourself

Being gentle with yourself means learning to laugh at the stupid things you do. Laughing at yourself and not taking life too seriously reflects a hopeful attitude and attracts scores of friends.

Think about your all-time most embarrassing moment. Describe it below (or on another piece of paper) as if you were writing it as a chapter in a dramatic novel. Make yourself the main character, describe the scene, add other characters (if any), and describe what you said and what you did.

Now take that same embarrassing moment and rewrite it as a stand-up comedian would describe it.

What are the differences in your two descriptions? After reading each one, do you feel differently about yourself or the embarrassing moment? Describe what you've noticed:

Learning to laugh at myself and my mistakes would help me have greater self-confidence because:

• BE HONEST

In the Personal Bank Account (PBA) chapter, you learn that being honest means being honest with yourself and being honest in your actions. Honesty is associated with words such as upstanding, incorruptible, moral, principled, truth-loving, steadfast, true, real, right, good, straight-shooting, and genuine. If you can apply these words to yourself, there's a good chance that you're an honest person.

Honesty means appearing to others as you really are. It means not being fake or trying to pass yourself off as something you're not. When you're not honest with yourself, you feel unsure and insecure, and you end up making a withdrawal from your PBA (the way you feel about yourself).

You can be honest in the activities you participate in every day. From taking tests to talking to parents and friends, to the things you do at work, you have constant opportunities to be honest or dishonest. Every act of honesty is a deposit into your PBA.

Describe an Honest Person

Read the Be Honest section on pages 38–39 of the *Teens* book.

The most honest person I know is: (This could be someone in your life, or a famous person you admire.)

He or she showed honesty by doing: (Describe the event or events.)

I can be more honest by: (List what you can do.)

● RENEW YOURSELF

You've gotta take time for yourself to renew and to relax. If you don't, you'll lose your zest for life. You might be familiar with the movie *The Secret Garden,* based on the book by Frances Hodgson Burnett. We all need a place we can escape to, a sanctuary of some sort, where we can renew our spirits. And it doesn't have to be a rose garden, mountaintop, or secluded beach. It can be a bedroom or even a bathroom, just a place to be alone.

Escape
Read the examples from other teens on page 40 of the *Teens* book.

The place I go to escape is:

What I want to remember about that place is: (Describe your escape place below.)

The place I wish was my escape place is:

The reason I wish it was my escape place is:

The characteristics of my escape place that make me go there when I'm stressed out, lonely, or sad are:

I feel better after I spend time in my escape place. True or false? (Why?)

If I can't go to my escape place, I do the following instead:

● TAP INTO YOUR TALENTS

Everyone has talents, whether you realize it or not. Talents are not just in sports, music, dance, or other more noticeable activities. The more important talents are within you. These talents could include reading, listening, being a fast learner, public speaking, loving others, having good organizational skills, cooking, caring for children, fixing cars, or being happy. It doesn't matter where your talents may lie. When you do something you love, it's exhilarating, and it can be a great deposit into your PBA.

Do Something Crazy

Have you ever watched those TV shows that search for the world's most talented person? Have you seen other shows that encourage you to send in a home video of yourself doing something outrageous? What if you had to send a video of yourself?

If a TV camera crew came to my home to film me doing a crazy talent, I would start doing:

My closest friend would say that my craziest talent is:

My closest friend's craziest talent is:

One thing I do well is: (Remember, talents can be things like speaking well in public, listening, being a good friend, etc.)

Hunt for your uniqueness. Ask someone you trust to describe what is unique about you. Describe what he or she said below.

The talent or unique trait I would develop if I didn't have limitations such as time, money, or physical ability is: (Brainstorm a plan where "the sky's the limit!")

The things I can use from my "dream plan" above to create a real-life plan are:

The things from my plan that I can start doing now are:

All of us are crazy
good in one way
or another.

—YIDDISH SAYING

Choose one or two Baby Steps you can do. Share your experiences with someone else, or write your experiences and learnings here.

Keep Promises to Yourself

 Get up when you planned to for three days in a row.

 Identify one easy task that needs to be done today, like putting in a batch of laundry or reading a book for an English assignment. Decide when you will do it. Now, keep your word and get it done.

Do Random Acts of Service

 Sometime today, do a kind anonymous deed, like writing a thank-you note, taking out the trash, or making someone's bed.

Look around and find something you can do to make a difference, like cleaning up a park in your neighborhood, volunteering in a senior citizens center, or reading to someone who can't.

Tap Into Your Talents

List a talent you would like to develop this year. Write down specific steps to get there.

Talent I want to develop this year: _____

How do I get there: _____

_____

_____

_____

Make a list of the talents you most admire in other people.

Person: Talents I Admire:

_____   _____

_____   _____

_____   _____

_____   _____

_____   _____

Be Gentle with Yourself

 Think about an area of life you feel inferior in. Now breathe deeply and tell yourself, "It's not the end of the world."

Try to go an entire day without negative self talk. Each time you catch yourself putting yourself down, you have to replace it with three positive thoughts about yourself.

Renew Yourself

Decide on a fun activity that will lift your spirits and do it today. For example, turn up the music and dance.

Feeling lethargic? Get up right now and go for a fast walk around the block.

Be Honest

The next time your parents ask you about what you're doing, share the complete story. Don't leave out information meant to mislead or deceive.

For one day, try not to exaggerate or embellish!

Which of the Baby Steps did I try, and what did I learn?

HABIT ①

Be
Proactive

I Am
the Force

You hit home runs not by chance but by preparation.

—ROGER MARIS

Proactive or Reactive . . . the Choice Is Yours

(A)re you a can of soda or a bottle of water? Reactive people make choices based on impulse. They are like a can of soda pop. If life shakes them up, the pressure builds and they explode.

Proactive people make choices based on values. They think before they act. They know that they can't control what happens to them in life, but they can control their response to what happens to them. Proactive people are like water. Shake them up all you want, take the lid off, and nothing. No explosion. They are cool, calm, and collected.

You may be a cross between the soda pop and the bottled water. We all have instances where we react or remain in control. You can usually tell the difference between reactive and proactive people by what they say. When you use reactive language, you give power to someone else willingly. You no longer have power over your emotions or actions.

Proactive language gives you back the control. You are free to choose who controls what you do and say. (It's *you!*)

Reactive ▼

So what is proactive behavior? Proactive behavior includes language such as:

- I'm sorry. I didn't mean that.
- I'll get right on that.
- I'm really not interested, but thank you.
- I'm sure we can think of a Third Alternative.
- I can.

▲ Proactive

But reactive behavior includes language such as:
- It's your fault.
- If only . . .
- I just can't decide.
- That's not fair.
- That's just the way I am.

I tend to be the most reactive: (When and where?)

I tend to be the most proactive: (When and where?)

The difficult challenge in life I'm faced with right now is:

I can face that challenge today and become a change agent by: (Describe your actions.)

● LISTEN TO YOUR LANGUAGE

In Habit 1: Be Proactive, you learn that you can usually hear the difference between proactive and reactive people by the language they use.

REACTIVE LANGUAGE	PROACTIVE LANGUAGE
I'll try.	*I'll do it.*
That's just the way I am.	*I can do better than that.*
There's nothing I can do.	*Let's look at all our options.*
I have to.	*I choose to.*
I can't.	*There's gotta be a way.*

REACTIVE LANGUAGE	PROACTIVE LANGUAGE
You ruined my day.	*I'm not going to let your bad mood rub off on me.*

When you use reactive language, it's like giving someone else the remote control to your life and saying, "Here, change my mood anytime you wish." Proactive language, on the other hand, puts the remote control back into your own hands. You are then free to choose which "channel" you want to be on.

I CAN'T HELP IT, MOM...IT'S JUST THE WAY I AM!

REACTIVE GUY

Evaluate Your Language

Read the Listen to Your Language section on page 51 of the *Teens* book. Complete the statements below:

I think my language is mostly: (Is it proactive or reactive?)

A phrase I use a lot that is proactive is:

A phrase I use a lot that is reactive is:

I can replace my reactive phrases with the following proactive phrases:

Someone in my life who is a really good example of how to use proactive language is:

The places or situations in my life where I tend to use proactive language are:

The places or situations in my life where I tend to use reactive language are:

AVOID THE VICTIMITIS VIRUS

Habit 1: Be Proactive explains that reactive people can suffer from a contagious virus called "victimitis." People infected with this disease believe that everyone has it in for them and that the world owes them something. Instead of recognizing that their attitude is the problem, reactive people are easily offended, blame others, get angry and say things they later regret, whine and complain, wait for things to happen to them, and change only when they have to.

A time when I felt like a victim was:

At the time, I felt I had a right to feel that way because:

Now that I know about the victimitis virus, I would do the following things differently in that situation:

IT PAYS TO BE PROACTIVE

Habit 1: Be Proactive teaches you that proactive people are a different breed. Proactive people:

Are not easily offended.

Take responsibility for their choices.

Think before they act.

Bounce back when something bad happens to them.

Always find a way to make it happen.

Focus on things they can do something about, and don't worry about things they can't.

As a result, proactive people are frequently rewarded for their efforts. They take control of their lives and have more freedom to do what they want. Proactive people draw others to them with their positive, can-do attitude.

Read the It Pays to Be Proactive section on pages 53–54 of the *Teens* book. In the space provided on the next page, draw your proactive self ten years from now.

- Draw a picture of yourself as you want to be in ten years.
- Draw a background. Where are you? Who is around you? What are you doing?
- Below the picture, list all of the positive attributes you possess as a proactive person.

• We Can Control Only One Thing

The fact is, you can't control everything that happens to you. As a teenager, this is especially true because your parents, teachers, and coaches seem to dictate your life. However, you can definitely control one thing: how you respond to what happens to you.

In Habit 1: Be Proactive, you learn about two circles. The inner circle is your Circle of Control. This circle includes things you have control over. The surrounding circle is the Circle of No Control. It contains the things you can't do anything about.

When you spend most of your time worrying about all the things you can't control, you feel even more out of control. When you focus on things you can control, you experience real control and find inner peace.

1. Read the We Can Control Only One Thing section that appears on pages 54–56 of the *Teens* book.
2. In the inner circle, list some of the things you can control in your life.
3. In the outer circle, list some of the things you can't control.

One thing in my Circle of No Control that I constantly worry about is:

I can stop worrying about that one thing by: (Describe your actions.)

TURN SETBACKS INTO TRIUMPHS

When life puts roadblocks in your way, can you find a solution? Do you think to go around or even over a huge obstacle in your path? Habit 1: Be Proactive explains that every setback is an opportunity for you to turn it into a triumph.

W. Mitchell was able to overcome not one but two horrific accidents that left him paralyzed and required skin grafts. Instead of worrying about what he no longer could do, he went on to become a millionaire, popular speaker, mayor, river rafter, and skydiver.

LOOK AT THIS AS AN OPPORTUNITY TO GROW.

W. Mitchell is a great example of turning setbacks into triumphs. He chose to be proactive and focus on the things he could control—his attitude.

Choose Your Reaction

Describe how you could turn a setback into a triumph for each of the following scenarios:

You and your best friend scope out others in the lunchroom every day. You point out to your friend a person that you would like to get to know better. The next day your friend tells you that he or she called and asked that person out last night.

The midsemester dance is next week. You and your friends are planning on going with another group and hanging out all night. You've been looking forward to it for a month. The day before the dance, you fall and break your leg and have a full-leg cast.

Having your own car is important to you. To keep it, you are working a job after school to pay the monthly car payments and insurance. Money is tight and you're barely making it, but still, you want a new car stereo. For six months, you have saved $15 from each paycheck toward the stereo. On your way home from work one night you are daydreaming and totally forget about the speed limit. You see flashing red lights in your rearview mirror. This speeding ticket is sure to cost at least as much as what you've saved for the stereo.

A setback I experienced or am currently experiencing is:

I could have turned or can turn that setback into a triumph by:

• RISE ABOVE ABUSE

In Habit 1: Be Proactive, you learn about turning setbacks into triumphs. One of the hardest setbacks is coping with abuse. If you have been abused, you need to recognize that you are not at fault. By being proactive, you won't have to live with the burden of your secret and your feelings of hopelessness for one more day.

You may ask yourself, "How can I be proactive after a situation like this?" The key to rising above abuse is seeking help. Abuse thrives in secrecy. By telling another person, you immediately divide your problem in half, which leads to healing and forgiving. If you have been abused, talk with someone today. Reach out to a loved one or a friend you can trust, take part in a help session, visit a professional therapist, or call an abuse hotline.

If you are friends with someone who has been abused, take the time to listen and offer help when that person reaches out to you. Above all, be sure to keep confidential the information that he or she shares with you.

Analyze Abuse

Read the Rising Above Abuse section on pages 58–59 of the *Teens* book.

If you have experienced abuse, complete the statement below:

I will be proactive by seeking help and reaching out to another person to share my secret of abuse. I will do this by: (Describe your plan.)

If you are the friend of someone who has been or is experiencing abuse, and he or she talks to you about his or her experience, complete the statement below:

I will take the time to listen and offer help by: (Describe your actions.)

If you know someone who has been or is experiencing abuse but has not come forward, complete the statement below:

I will reach out to that person as a friend. I will take time to show him or her that I care and that I am trustworthy. I will do this by: (Describe your actions.)

To begin taking the first steps away from abuse, please see the list of hotlines on page 250 of the *Teens* book.

● BECOME A CHANGE AGENT

Harmful habits such as abuse, alcoholism, and welfare dependency are often passed down from parents to kids. As a result, dysfunctional families keep repeating themselves. Even habits that aren't so bad but limit you are passed down and prohibit you from becoming the best you can be.

> Whether I fail or succeed shall be no man's doing but my own. I am the force.
>
> —ELAINE MAXWELL

Habit 1: Be Proactive teaches that you can stop the cycle and reach your potential. When you are proactive, you stop bad or limiting habits from being passed on. You become a "change agent" and pass on good habits to future generations, starting with your own kids. You have the power within you to rise above whatever may have been passed down to you.

Stop the Cycle

Read the Becoming a Change Agent section on pages 59–61 of the *Teens* book. Complete the statements below:

One habit that has been passed down to me that I would like to change or improve is:

The history of that bad habit is: (Describe where it came from and how it has affected your family's life.)

This bad habit has affected my life in these ways:

By changing that bad habit, my life will be different in these ways:

To change that bad habit, I can do the following every day: (Describe your actions.)

● GROW YOUR PROACTIVE MUSCLES

Habit 1: Be Proactive encourages you to change your frame of mind from reactive (making choices based on impulse) to proactive (making choices based on values). As you strengthen your proactive muscles, you are better able to take responsibility for your life and help and influence others.

NOTHING CAN HURT "PROACTIVE MAN"!

Take Responsibility

Read the poem "Five Short Chapters" on page 62 of the *Teens* book. Complete the activity below:

1. Find a friend to help you complete this activity. Have your friend blindfold you.
2. Have your friend stand at one end of a room filled with furniture or a yard with obstacles.
3. As you walk toward your friend, have him or her tell you "hot" or "cold" to help you avoid the obstacles. (Note: Be careful not to use anything that could hurt you or that you could damage.)
4. When you reach your friend, have him or her lead you back to your starting place.
5. Repeat the activity.

The second time you walked toward your friend, was it easier to avoid the obstacles?

> To be a hero or a heroine, one must give an order to oneself.
> —SIMONE WEIL

What did you do differently the second time?

What knowledge did you have the second time that you didn't have the first? Did that knowledge help you proactively avoid the obstacles? How?

Even though your friend was trying to keep you away from the obstacles, did you accidentally bump into them? How is that like reactive behavior?

What could you have done during the activity to proactively avoid the obstacles?

● CAN-DO

American aviator Elinor Smith once said, "It has long since come to my attention that people of accomplishment rarely sat back and let things happen to them. They went out and happened to things."

Habit 1: Be Proactive discusses that can-do people use initiative, creativity, and courage to make things happen. Can-do people don't wait for life to happen to them. They go out and work for what they want.

Think of a Can-Do Person

Read the Can-Do section on pages 63–65 of the *Teens* book.

A can-do person I admire is: (He or she can be someone famous or an acquaintance.)

This person is a can-do person because: (Describe what tells you that he or she has this attitude.)

This can-do attitude helped the person overcome the following obstacles:

By having a can-do attitude, this person has had the following successes:

If this person didn't have a can-do attitude, his or her life would be different in the following ways:

An obstacle in my life that is preventing me from accomplishing my goals is:

I can use the can-do approach to overcome this obstacle by: (Describe your actions.)

JUST PUSH PAUSE

Sometimes life moves so fast that you instantly react to everything out of sheer habit. If you can learn to "just push pause," get control, and think about how you want to respond, you'll make smarter decisions.

Habit 1: Be Proactive explains that while you are pausing, you can use four human tools to help you decide what to do. These tools are:

Self-awareness: I can stand apart from myself and observe my thoughts and actions.

Conscience: I can listen to my inner voice to know right from wrong.

Imagination: I can envision new possibilities.

Willpower: I have the power to choose.

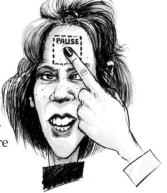

You either use or fail to use your four human tools every day of your life. The more you use them, the stronger they become and the more power you have to Be Proactive.

See How Well You Use Your Pause Button

Read the Just Push Pause section on pages 65–68 of the *Teens* book. See how well you use your pause button and your human tools by answering the statements below:

N = Never   S = Sometimes   A = Always

SELF-AWARENESS

I take time to examine my thoughts or feelings and change them if necessary.	N	S	A
I am aware of how my thoughts affect my attitude and behavior.	N	S	A
I take time to quietly ponder and think without interruptions.	N	S	A

CONSCIENCE

I get a feeling inside me that prompts me about things I should or shouldn't do.	N	S	A
I listen to the feelings that prompt me and behave accordingly.	N	S	A

HABIT 1

N = Never   S = Sometimes   A = Always

CONSCIENCE (*continued*)

I have taken time to think about what I value.

| N | S | A |

I can tell the difference between what society and the media want me to value and what my own values are.

| N | S | A |

IMAGINATION

I think ahead.

| N | S | A |

I have pictured myself succeeding in my goals.

| N | S | A |

I can easily imagine other solutions to problems or obstacles.

| N | S | A |

WILLPOWER

I make and keep promises to myself and others.

| N | S | A |

I set and achieve meaningful goals in my life.

| N | S | A |

I remember and honor my values in the moment of choice.

| N | S | A |

When you have completed the questionnaire, go back and review your answers. Ask yourself, "Do I use my pause button enough? If not, how can I improve?"

Read the scenario below and answer the questions that follow.

You've been working on the school yearbook and have been extremely committed and dependable. Three months ago, a new student joined the staff. Recently, he was given the title of Yearbook Editor, the job you'd been hoping for.

What are some proactive choices you could make in this situation by pressing pause and using each of your four human tools, rather than reacting based on your habits or emotions?

 Self-awareness:

 Conscience:

 Imagination:

 Willpower:

● PUT HUMAN TOOLS IN ACTION

Sometimes you don't think about what you're doing; you just do it. Someone pushes you and you push back. Your reactions are impulses with little thought as to the consequences. Habit 1: Be Proactive

> What happens is not as important as how you react to what happens.
>
> —ELLEN GLASGOW

tells you that if you can learn to pause, get control, and think about how you want to respond, you'll make smarter decisions.

To make smarter decisions, use your toolbox of four human tools.

1. Read the Human Tools in Action section on pages 68–70 of the *Teens* book.
2. Choose one of the human tools.
3. Imagine that you are a personal trainer for the human tool that you chose.
4. See the example planner sheet below.
5. On the blank pages provided, design your own training program on Planner pages to strengthen that human tool.

Example

Weekly Goals

My Big Rocks
Study for science test
Finish reading book
Attend Megan's game
Complete employment application
Party at Isabella's
Exercise 3 times

STUDY TIP: Don't tie yourself down to one career choice. It is a wise idea to have some different options.

"Noise proves nothing. Often a hen who has merely laid an egg cackles as if she laid an asteroid." MARK TWAIN

SUNDAY 10 JANUARY

Finish reading book

MONDAY 11 JANUARY

1:00 Lift weights
Science test-study

British invasion: The Beatles release their first album, Love Me Do, 1962.

TUESDAY 12 JANUARY

Science test-study

WEDNESDAY 13 JANUARY
7:00 Aerobics

6:30 Megan's Game

THURSDAY 14 JANUARY

FRIDAY 15 JANUARY
7:00 Aerobics

8:00 Party at Isabella's

SATURDAY 16 JANUARY
Complete employment application

HABIT
1

Choose one or two Baby Steps you can do. Share your experiences with someone else, or write your experiences and learnings here.

 The next time someone flips you off, give them the peace sign back.

 Listen carefully to your words today. Count how many times you use reactive language, such as "You make me . . . ," "I have to . . . ," "Why can't they . . . ," "I can't . . ."

Reactive language I use most: _____

_____

_____

_____

 Do something today that you have wanted to do but never dared. Leave your comfort zone and go for it. Ask someone out on a date, raise your hand in class, or join a team.

 Write yourself a Post-it note: "I will not let _____

_____

decide how I'm going to feel." Place it in your locker, on your mirror, or in your planner and refer to it often.

 At the next party, don't just sit against the wall and wait for excitement to find you, you find it. Walk up and introduce yourself to someone new.

The next time you receive a grade that you think is unfair, don't blow it off or cry about it, make an appointment with the teacher to discuss it and then see what you can learn.

If you get in a fight with a parent or a friend, be the first to apologize.

 Identify something in your circle of no control that you are always worrying about. Decide now to drop it.

Thing that I can't control that I always worry about:

_____

_____

Push the pause button before you react to someone who bumps into you in the hall, calls you a name, or cuts in line.

Use your tool of self-awareness right now by asking yourself, "What is my most unhealthy habit?" Make up your mind to do something about it.

Most unhealthy habit: _____

_____

What I'm going to do about it: _____

_____

_____

_____

Which of the Baby Steps did I try, and what did I learn?

HABIT 2

Begin with the **End in Mind**

Control Your **Own Destiny**

OR SOMEONE ELSE WILL

The paths you choose now can affect you forever.
—SEAN COVEY

Begin with the End in Mind—What It Means

H abit 2: Begin with the End in Mind means developing a clear picture of where you want to go in life. It means deciding what your values and principles are and setting goals for yourself. Habit 1 says you're the driver, not just the passenger. Habit 2 says that since you're the driver, decide on your destination and then create a map to get there.

To begin with the end in mind, you don't need to decide every little detail right now. That would take some fun out of the trip. Simply, if you think beyond today and decide in what direction you want your life to go, it's more than likely that each step will get you closer to that goal.

You already do it all the time. Don't you create an outline before you do a research paper? A recipe before you bake a cake? Map before you take a road trip to Disneyland?

• CROSSROADS OF LIFE

As a teen, you benefit hugely from having an end in mind because you are at a critical crossroads in your life. The paths you choose now affect your future.

At which crossroads of life are you standing right now? Which roads do you feel you are choosing (for example, college, marriage, family, career, armed forces, professional athlete, good health, money, etc.)?

Fill in your answers on the crossroads sign to the right.

CROSSROADS OF LIFE

Daily you face questions about these issues that will affect your future beginning right now. Decide now how you will respond to these questions before you face them and have to decide without thinking.

- Schoolwork: (Drop out or stay in school? Do as little work as possible and just get by? Begin scholarship applications today or put them off? Decide on a college or have someone decide for you?)

- Sex: (Have sex or abstain? Cave in to pressure from your boyfriend or girlfriend? Not have sex and talk as if you do?)

- Drugs: (Take drugs or not? Experiment or not? Cave in to peer pressure or not? Drink and drive or be the designated driver? Not do drugs but talk as if you do? Smoke or not? Assist others in doing drugs or not?)

WHAT ABOUT FRIENDS?

Habit 2: Begin with the End in Mind teaches that the paths you choose today can shape you forever. If you join a gang, the things you do may affect you for the rest of your life. If you smoke, drink, or do drugs, how will your health be affected several years down the road?

What values will you choose? What will you stand for? How will you contribute to the community? Believe it or not, answers to these questions depend on what you do and the decisions you make as a teenager.

The friends you choose can really affect the choices you make. Friends can help you or hurt you. They will seriously influence your attitude, reputation, and direction, so choose them wisely.

Read the Crossroads of Life—What About Friends? section that appears on pages 76–78 of the *Teens* book. Complete the following statements about your friends.

My best friends and friends I hang out with are: (Write their names.)

The fun stuff we like to do together is:

The interests we have in common are:

● WHAT ABOUT SEX?

Habit 2: Begin with the End in Mind teaches that the decision you make about sex will affect your health, your self-image, how fast you grow up, your reputation, whom you marry, your future children, and so much more. You are free to choose your path, but you can't choose the consequences that come with it.

Read The Crossroads of Life—What About Sex? section on page 78 of the *Teens* book. Answer the questions below (taken from the U.S. Department of Health and Human Services).

	YES	NO
Does having sex agree with your moral values?		
Would your parents approve of you having sex now?		
If you have a child, are you responsible enough to provide for its emotional and financial support?		
If the relationship breaks up, will you be glad you had sex with your partner?		
Are you sure no one is pushing you into having sex?		
Does your partner want to have sex now?		
Are you absolutely sure your partner is not infected with a sexually transmitted disease (STD), including HIV/AIDS?		

If any of your answers to these questions is no, then you'd better wait. You'll learn more about making this tough decision when you get to Habit 7.

Choose one of the things you listed on the crossroads sign on page 64 of this workbook and think about how your decision will affect your:

Health:

Self-image:

Reputation:

Choice of whom to marry:

Future children:

● WHAT ABOUT SCHOOL?

Habit 2: Begin with the End in Mind teaches that what you decide about your schooling now can shape your future in a major way. Whether you realize it or not, you have the entire world in front of you at this time in your life. You can achieve whatever you want. You can go as far as you want to go. But a large part of that is tied to the decisions you make about school. So choose wisely, and don't limit your options by selling yourself short.

Learn from Someone Else

Read The Crossroads of Life—What About School? section that appears on pages 79–80 of the *Teens* book.

Someone I know who values education and learning in school is:

Interview the person you named above and ask him or her the following six questions.

1. When you were a teenager, what did you plan to be when you "grew up"?

2. When you were a teenager, what was your educational plan (attend college, trade school, etc.)?

3. Where did you go to high school? Where did you go to college?

4. How have your experiences in high school affected your life so far?

5. How have your experiences in college affected your life so far?

6. Do you wish you had made a different educational plan? If yes, what do you wish you had done?

Postinterview Questions for You

My interviewee's answer that surprised me the most was:

Other answers or things that surprised me were:

The advice I would like to take away from interviewing this person is:

When I "grow up," I plan to be:

Doing well in school will affect that goal because:

My educational plan (attend college, trade school, etc.) is:

The college, trade school, etc., that I plan to attend is:

The experiences in high school that could affect the rest of my life are:

WHO'S IN THE LEAD?

Habit 2: Begin with the End in Mind teaches that if you don't create a vision of your own, someone else will do it for you—friends, parents, the media, or someone else. And who knows if their interests are the same as yours? Unless you create your own vision of who and what you want to be, you will be quick to follow anyone who is willing to lead, even into things that won't get you very far.

Read the Who's in the Lead? section on page 80 of the *Teens* book. Think about your vision of the future, including where, what, and who you want to be. Complete the statements below.

Having a vision of who and where I want to be in the future is important because:

The consequences of not having a vision are:

Choosing friends who have the same values I believe in is important because:

Some things my friends value are:

Some things my parents and family value are:

My values that are the same as those of my friends and family are:

The consequences of choosing friends who have different values than my own are:

The choices I make as a teenager can affect me when I'm older in the following ways:

CRAFT YOUR OWN PERSONAL MISSION STATEMENT

A Personal Mission Statement is like a personal credo or motto that states what your life is about. It is the blueprint for building your life. It is the map for life's journey. Since your destiny is yet to be decided, why not decide today to make it extraordinary and leave a lasting legacy?

Remember, life is a mission, not a career. A career is a profession. A career asks, "What's in it for me?" A mission asks, "How can I make a difference?"

A Personal Mission Statement is important for me because:

Complete The Great Discovery worksheet on the next pages.

Start here!

1 Think of a person who made a positive difference in your life. What qualities does that person have that you would like to develop?

_____

_____

_____

_____

2 Imagine yourself in twenty years. You are surrounded by the most important people in your life. Who are they and what are you doing?

_____

_____

_____

_____

_____

_____

_____

3 If a steel beam (six inches wide) were placed across two skyscrapers, for what would you be willing to cross? A thousand dollars? A million? Your pet? Your brother? Fame? Think carefully.

_____

_____

_____

6 Describe a time when you were deeply inspired.

_____
_____
_____
_____
_____
_____

5 List ten things you love to do. It could be singing, dancing, looking at magazines, drawing, reading, daydreaming—anything you absolutely love to do.

1 _____
2 _____
3 _____
4 _____
5 _____
6 _____
7 _____
8 _____
9 _____
10 _____

THE ROMAN EMPIRE OR ANYTHING HISTO

4

If you could spend one day in a great library studying anything you wanted, what would you study?

_____
_____
_____

7 Five years from now, your local paper does a story about you, and the reporter wants to interview three people—a parent, a brother or sister, and a friend. What would you want them to say about you?

_____

_____

_____

_____

8 Think of something that represents you—a rose, a song, an animal. Why does it represent you?

_____

_____

_____

_____

_____

E=MC²

9 If you could spend an hour with any person who ever lived, who would that be? Why that person? What would you ask?

_____

_____

_____

_____

HEY, LOOK WHAT I FOUND. IT'S **ME!**

Numbers
Words
Creative thinking
Athletics
Making things happen
Sensing needs   Speaking
Mechanical   Writing
Artistic   Dancing
Working with people   Listening
Memorizing things   Singing
Decision making   Humor
Building things   Sharing
Predicting what will happen Music
Accepting others   Trivia

10 Everyone has one or more talents. What are your talents? Use the ones listed or write your own.

_____   _____
_____   _____
_____   _____
_____   _____

HABIT 2

• DISCOVER YOUR TALENTS

Habit 2: Begin with the End in Mind teaches that an important part of developing a Personal Mission Statement is discovering what you're good at. Everyone has a talent, gift, or something he or she is good at. The secret is figuring out what it is.

Some talents attract a lot of attention, like being a great athlete or singer. Others may not grab as much attention but are just as important. Being skilled at listening, making people laugh, giving, forgiving, drawing, or just being nice are talents that make the world a better place.

Name Your Talents

1. Read the Uncovering Your Talents section on pages 83–84 of the *Teens* book.
2. Choose three people who know you well.
3. Interview the three people you have chosen. Ask them to identify at least three talents they think you have.
4. List the name of each person and the talents he or she described in the spaces below.

Person 1:

1. _____
2. _____
3. _____

Person 2:

1. _____
2. _____
3. _____

Person 3:

1. _____
2. _____
3. _____

5. Circle the talents you didn't realize you had.

• GET STARTED ON YOUR MISSION STATEMENT

Habit 2: Begin with the End in Mind teaches that there are as many ways to write a mission statement as there are people in the world. The important part is to write something that inspires you—something that reminds you of your values, your standards, and the things you want to achieve in your life.

Read the Getting Started on Your Mission Statement section that appears on pages 90–91 of the *Teens* book.

Write the name of a famous person.

Answer the questions below.

What is/was important to this person?

What inspires/inspired this person?

What is a brief mission statement for the famous person you chose?

What are some of the qualities you admire most in others?

Review the last two pages above and The Great Discovery worksheet. Set a timer for five minutes and start writing your Personal Mission Statement. Write fast—don't stop to worry about or rewrite what you're writing. Just write down all the ideas that come to mind. Don't worry if it seems disjointed or untidy. If you can't think of what to write, write, "I can't think of anything." Just keep writing!

You can also refer to the sample Personal Mission Statement below if you need help.

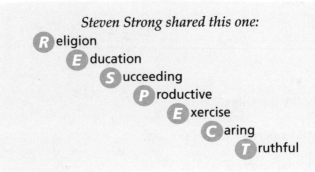

Steven Strong shared this one:

R eligion
  E ducation
    S ucceeding
      P roductive
        E xercise
          C aring
            T ruthful

THREE WATCH-OUTS

Habit 2: Begin with the End in Mind teaches that labels are an ugly form of prejudice. When you label someone, you make unfair conclusions—often without truly knowing him or her first. Most of you are labeled at one time or another in life, but the danger comes when you start to believe the labels.

Labels are like paradigms. What you see is what you get. For instance, if you've been labeled as lazy, and you begin to believe it yourself, it becomes a self-fulfilling belief. You'll act out the label. Just remember, you are not your labels.

Examine What You Notice

Read the Three Watch-Outs section on pages 92–94 of the *Teens* book.

Imagine you are walking down the hallway in your school. A girl whom you've never seen before is walking in the opposite direction.

Most likely, the first thing I'll notice about her is:

Does what I notice about her make me give her an instant label? Why?

What if my observation about that girl is not right? How can I mentally remove that label?

A label I have put on someone in the past is:

I gave that person the label because:

That label affected the way I treated him or her because:

Another way that label may have affected him or her is:

● GO FOR THE GOAL

Habit 2: Begin with the End in Mind teaches you that goals are more specific than a mission statement. In fact, goals can help you break down your mission into bite-size pieces. A mission statement is what you want to accomplish; goals are how you're going to accomplish it.

Make It Real

Read the Go for the Goal section on pages 94–98 of the *Teens* book. Then complete the statements below.

One goal I would like to achieve is:

Count the cost—One or two things I may have to give up to achieve this goal are:

1. _____

2. _____

The benefits I will receive from giving up these things are:

Put It in Pen—I will write down my goal in the following special place:

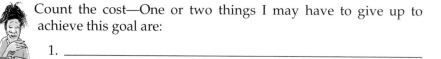

Some specific things I need to do or remember about this goal are:

Just Do It—I will commit to achieving this goal by using these reminders to myself:

Use Momentous Moments—the changes I've made to my life as a result of momentous events are: (Review the list of momentous events on page 97 of the *Teens* book.)

Through those momentous event changes, I learned these things about myself:

Rope Up—The main person who can help me achieve my goal is:

Other people who can help me achieve my goal are:

One famous person (past or present) I wish could help me with my goal is:

His or her qualities that would help me achieve the goal are:

GOALS IN ACTION

Habit 2: Begin with the End in Mind teaches that goals help you get where you want to go. Without goals, you will likely stray from your path and miss your destination. Goals help you stay on course and make sure you get where you're going in the shortest amount of time.

Read the Goals in Action section on pages 98–101 of the *Teens* book. Complete the statements below about how goals helped David.

Goals helped David get where he wanted to go because:

Some things that might have happened if David hadn't set goals are:

Now answer these questions for yourself.

My life can be different by setting goals because:

Setting goals helps me Begin with the End in Mind by:

HABIT 2

TURN WEAKNESSES INTO STRENGTHS

How many times do you wish you could be someone else? Do you ever think thoughts like "If I only had her curly hair . . ." or "If I could only play football like him . . ." or "If I could only sing like that . . ."?

Habit 2: Begin with the End in Mind teaches that weaknesses can actually make you stronger. When you think you lack the physical, social, or mental gifts you want, just fight that much harder to reach your goals. And that uphill battle gives you qualities and strengths you couldn't develop any other way.

That is how you make a weakness a strength.

Form a Plan

Read the Turning Weaknesses into Strengths section on pages 101–102 of the *Teens* book. My weaknesses and strengths are: (List them in the table below.)

MY STRENGTHS	MY WEAKNESSES
I am a loyal friend.	*I quickly jump to conclusions.*

Of my weaknesses above, I can take the following steps to turn one of my weaknesses into a strength:

● MAKE YOUR LIFE EXTRAORDINARY

Habit 2: Begin with the End in Mind encourages you to make your life extraordinary.

Since your destiny is yet to be determined, why not make it extraordinary and leave a lasting legacy? You don't have to change the world to have a mission. You just

> Strength does not come from physical capacity. It comes from an indomitable will.
>
> —MOHANDAS GANDHI

need to take advantage of and seek out opportunities to be your best self.

Learn from Example

Read the Make Your Life Extraordinary section on pages 102–103 of the *Teens* book.

The legacy I want to leave is:

(Read the quote by Greg Anderson below.) The place where I most focus my attention is:

The place I named in the question above is where I want to leave a legacy. True or false?

If false, I will start focusing my life on the following to leave the legacy I want to leave by:

> Only one thing has to change for us to know happiness in our lives: where we focus our attention.
>
> —GREG ANDERSON

Choose one or two Baby Steps you can do. Share your experiences with someone else, or write your experiences and learnings here.

 Determine the three most important skills you'll need to succeed in your career. Do you need to be more organized, be more confident speaking in front of other people, have stronger writing skills?

The three most important skills I need for my career:

_____

_____

_____

 Review your mission statement daily for 30 days (that's how long it takes to develop a habit). Let it guide you in all your decisions.

 Look in the mirror and ask, "Would I want to marry someone like me?" If not, work to develop the qualities you're lacking.

 Go to your school guidance or employment counselor and talk about career opportunities. Take an aptitude test that will help you evaluate your talents, abilities, and interests.

 What is the key crossroad you are facing in your life right now? In the long run, what is the best path to take?

Key crossroad I am facing: _____

_____

The best path to take:_____

_____

Make a copy of The Great Discovery. Then take a friend or family member through it step by step.

Think about your goals. Have you put them in pen and written them down? If not, take time to do it. Remember, a goal not written is only a wish.

Identify a negative label others may have given you. Think up a few things you can do to change that label.

Negative label: _____

How to change it: _____

Which of the Baby Steps did I try, and what did I learn?

HABIT ③

Put **First Things** First

Will and Won't **Power**

I must govern the clock, not be governed by it.

—GOLDA MEÎR

Pack More into Your Life

You've got a lot to do, and you're faced with more decisions and choices than any group of teens in history. A regular day typically goes like this: You get up early and practice your music, and then you're off to school. Your top three college choices are due today, and a scholarship deadline is looming. Your chemistry homework is not done, and after school you have ball practice. You're supposed to work tonight, and you promised your brother you'd take him out for ice cream. Oh, and you have a date planned for the weekend, but you have no idea what you're going to do. Where do you begin?

Quadrant 1: The Procrastinator

To practice Habit 3: Put First Things First, you need to manage your time and avoid putting things off until the last minute. Habit 3 explains that you manage your time in four different time quadrants. Each quadrant contains different kinds of activities, which are broken into a combination of two categories: urgent and important.

If you spend too much time in Quadrant 1 (urgent and important tasks), you become stressed out and anxious, you may not do your best, and you may disappoint yourself and others. Some people thrive on deadlines. Doing everything at the last minute gives them a rush. They won't even begin a task until it becomes urgent. Are you a chronic procrastinator addicted to urgency?

Read the Packing More into Your Life—Quadrant 1: The Procrastinator section on pages 107–108 of the *Teens* book.

Now, honestly answer the questions in the following table.

	TRUE	FALSE
I frequently grab fast food or junk or skip meals because I don't have time to sit down to a real meal.		
I cram for tests the night before.		
I write papers the night before they are due. I rarely read through them before I turn them in.		
I frequently arrive late to appointments, practice, school, etc.		
I am not good at planning or organizing.		
I can't seem to get motivated without pressure being applied.		
I am frequently preoccupied with one thing while I am doing something else.		
I feel frustrated by the slowness of people and things around me; I hate to wait or stand in line.		
I seem to rush between places and events.		
I rarely have time (or save time) for myself.		
I frequently wish I had thought about things and acted sooner. Often, I am just too late.		
I miss friends' and family birthdays.		
I frequently miss assignments or appointments.		
Totals		

"True" Scores:

10–13 You definitely have an urgency problem.

   7–9 You are a moderate procrastinator.

   1–6 You may have some urgency tendencies, but they are manageable.

Quadrant 3: The Yes-Man

Quadrant 3 represents activities that are urgent but not important. People who spend their time in this quadrant typically try to please others and have a hard time saying no. If you spend too much time in Quadrant 3, you may lack discipline.

Read the Packing More into Your Life—Quadrant 3: The Yes-Man section on pages 109–110 of the *Teens* book.

One way to fill your precious time with worthwhile activities is to identify your most important priorities right now. Then, you can do the activities first that support those priorities.

List two of your highest priorities on the left side of the table below. On the right side of the table, list the activities you'll turn down to fulfill that priority.

HIGH PRIORITY	ACTIVITY I WILL TURN DOWN TO FULFILL MY HIGH PRIORITY
Academic scholarship	*After-school activities*
	Social events
	Television
	Extra shifts at work
_____	_____
_____	_____

Quadrant 2: The Prioritizer

Quadrant 2 is made up of activities like relaxing, building friendships, exercising, planning ahead, and doing homework. It's the quadrant of excellence—the place to be.

Habit 3: Put First Things First teaches that the key to effective time management is to shift as much time as possible into Quadrant 2. The only way you'll find more time for Quadrant 2 is to reduce the amount of time you spend in the other quadrants.

Assess Quadrant Time

1. Read the Packing More into Your Life—Quadrant 2: The Prioritizer section on pages 111–112 of the *Teens* book.
2. Complete the assessment at the top of the next page.
3. Add up the totals in the space provided.
4. Using the scoring table, locate the total for each quadrant in the "Score" column and identify the accompanying percentage in the "%" column.
5. Fill in the percentage for each quadrant in the Time Quadrants table.

Never = 1   Always = 5

1. How often during my typical day do I fix problems?

   1   2   3   4   5

2. How often during my typical day do I work to improve study skills?

   1   2   3   4   5

3. How often during my typical day do I drop what I'm doing to hang out with friends who call or stop by?

   1   2   3   4   5

4. How often during my typical day do I watch TV, play video games, or surf the Web?

   1   2   3   4   5

5. How often during my typical day do I deal with emergencies?

   1   2   3   4   5

6. How often during my typical day do I spend time with my siblings or other family members?

   1   2   3   4   5

7. How often during my typical day do I do things other people want me to do?

   1   2   3   4   5

8. How often during my day do I hang out and chat?

   1   2   3   4   5

Questions 1 and 5 (Quadrant 1): ☐

Questions 2 and 6 (Quadrant 2): ☐

Questions 3 and 7 (Quadrant 3): ☐

SCORING TABLE   Questions 4 and 8 (Quadrant 4): ☐

Score	%
10	45
9	40
8	35
7	30
6	25
5	20
4	15
3	10
2	5

TIME QUADRANTS

	URGENT	NOT URGENT
IMPORTANT	① % Urgent. I HAVE to do it or something bad will happen.	② % Important to my life dreams and goals.
NOT IMPORTANT	③ % Seems urgent, but if I skipped it, nothing bad would happen.	④ % Not terribly important. Not urgent either. Time wasters.

● PICK UP A PLANNER

Habit 3: Put First Things First is about learning to prioritize and manage your time so that your first things (highest priorities) come first, not last. You may have a nice list of goals and good intentions, but doing them—putting them first—is the really hard part.

Putting first things first also deals with learning to overcome your fears and being strong during hard moments. Habit 3 is the habit of "will power" (the strength to say yes to your most important things) and "won't power" (the strength to say no to less important things and to peer pressure).

Time Your Tasks

1. Read the Pick Up a Planner section on pages 112–116 of the *Teens* book.
2. Complete the survey on the next page by writing how many hours you think you spend on each item in an average week.

TASK	HOURS SPENT
Attending classes	
Attending religious activities	
Doing chores	
Doing extracurricular activities (lessons, sports, etc.)	
Doing homework	
Dressing/hygiene	
Eating	
Going to appointments	
Sleeping	
Spending leisure time	
Spending time with family	
Spending time with friends	
Studying	
Traveling	
Volunteering	
Working	
Other	
Total	

Do I actually have more to do in a day than I have time?

The things that take up most of my time are (school, watching TV, reading, hanging out):

The things that fill up my average day are the things that matter most to me. True or false?

The thing I waste the most time on is:

With all the stuff you have going on in your life and all the things you have to do, it's a good idea for you to use a planner or some sort of calendar. You've got to have a place to write down your assignments, appointments, to-do lists, special dates, and goals, or something will slip between the cracks.

● PLAN WEEKLY

Each week you have important things you've got to get done. These things could include studying for a big test, finishing a reading assignment, attending a friend's game, exercising, practicing for a recital or  concert, or applying for a job. These are your "Big Rocks"—the most important things you need to do during the week.

 In Habit 3: Put First Things First, you learn that if you plan the Big Rocks in your life first, everything fits—Big Rocks *and* pebbles, which are your less important tasks.

● PICK THE BIG ROCKS

Take fifteen minutes at the beginning or end of every week and decide what you want to accomplish in the upcoming week. Ask yourself, "What are the most important things I need to do?" These are your Big Rocks for the upcoming week—your mini-goals that help you live your mission statement (remember Habit 2) and lead you to achieve your long-term goals.

Read the Pick Up a Planner—Plan Weekly section on pages 113–115 of the *Teens* book.

My Big Rocks for the upcoming week are:

I will schedule them into my week by: (Describe your planning system or actions.)

● EXAMINE YOUR ROLES

Did you know you play many roles in your life, such as student, brother or sister, son or daughter, sports team member, club member, church member, grandchild, employee, etc.?

In Habit 3: Put First Things First, you learn to determine and think through the key roles in your life and come up with one or two important things you want to get done in each role.

Planning your life around roles will help you stay balanced. Think about your roles as you plan your day. That way you'll spend time in the areas that are most important to you and lead to great results.

HABIT **3**

Set Goals for Each Role

The roles I play in my life are: (For example: student, friend, family member, employee, debate team member, etc.)

1. In the table below, list your most important roles in the left-hand column.
2. Ask yourself, "If I were to do one thing this week that would make a difference in this role, what would it be?"
3. Write one thing that would make a difference in the right-hand column next to each role you have identified.

ROLE	ONE THING TO MAKE A DIFFERENCE
Student	*Study for science test.*
Family member	*Call grandma.*

As you plan this week, block out time for your "one thing" in each role in your planner. For example, you might decide that the best time to call your grandma is Sunday afternoon. So block out that time in your planner. It's like making a reservation. If your goal doesn't have a specific time attached to it, chances are you won't get it done.

Plan a Future Event

1. Refer to the Pick Up a Planner—Plan Weekly section on pages 113–115 of the *Teens* book.
2. To help you begin with the end in mind, imagine you are at a family gathering or high school reunion ten years from now with the people who are closest to you. If they could each say something about you, what would you want them to say?
3. In the table on the next page, write the name

of the person and his or her relationship to you on the left side (for example: family member, friend, classmate, coworker, church or community leader, teacher, etc.).

4. On the right side, write down what you would like him or her to say about you. (Remember, put what you want this person to say about you, even if it doesn't reflect your current behavior.)

PERSON	STATEMENT ABOUT YOU
Jane, best friend	*She always lifted me up and was there for me during the hard times.*

One of my important roles that I would like to focus on more is:

One thing I will do this week to pay more attention to that role is:

THE OTHER HALF

Managing your time is only the first half of Habit 3. The other half is learning to overcome peer pressure. Some of the hardest moments come when you face peer pressure. Saying no when all your friends are saying yes takes raw courage. Sometimes, peer pressure can be so strong, the only way to resist it is to completely get away from the situation or environment you're in.

Find Your First Things

Read The Other Half—Overcoming Peer Pressure section that appears on pages 123–125 of the *Teens* book.

Three things that should come first in my life are:

1. _____

2. _____

3. _____

Of the three things I listed, the one that comes first in my life is:

This one thing is so valuable to me because:

Peer pressure affects my ability to put this one thing first in these ways:

I can resist peer pressure by: (Describe your actions.)

Beginning with the end in mind can help me put my first thing first because:

The first time I stood up for something I believed in, despite the fact that I stood alone, was:

Here's what happened:

• DON'T LET YOUR FEARS DECIDE

The world is full of emotions, but perhaps one of the worst is fear. Think about some experiences you may have missed in life because your fears got the best of you. Fears whisper, "You can't do it," or "They may not like you." Ugly, yet very real, fears can prevent you from taking classes, making friends, or playing for teams.

Try to remember this quote when you think you might cave in to your fears: "Never let your fears make your decisions. *You* make them." Acting in the face of fear is never easy, but afterward you'll be glad you did.

Face Your Fears

Some things I am comfortable doing are:

Some things that are easy for me but may seem difficult or frightening to someone else are: (For example: making friends, skateboarding, etc.)

HABIT 3

I am afraid of these things:

Things that require courage for me to do are:

The worst thing that could happen if I faced this fear is:

The best thing that could happen if I faced this fear is: (Imagine how good you would feel to be free of the burden.)

(Read The Other Half—The Comfort Zone and the Courage Zone section on pages 117–118 of the *Teens* book.) Some things that hold me back from moving into my courage zone are:

One thing that's outside my comfort zone that I am going to act on today is:

- ## THE COMMON INGREDIENT OF SUCCESS

Habit 3: Put First Things First teaches that putting first things first takes discipline. It takes discipline to manage your time. It takes discipline to overcome your fears. It takes discipline to be strong in the hard moments and resist peer pressure.

> To conquer fear is the beginning of wisdom.
>
> —BERTRAND RUSSELL

   A man named Albert E. Gray spent years studying successful people to try to figure out the special ingredient that made them all successful. What do you think he found? Well, it wasn't dressing for success, or eating bran, or having a positive mental attitude. Instead, this is what he found. Read it carefully.

Shoot for Success
Read The Common Ingredient of Success section on pages 125–126 of the *Teens* book.

Something I would like to achieve that requires a lot of hard work or sacrifice is: (For example, become a concert pianist, discover gold, etc.)

Five steps I need to do to accomplish my goal are: (For example, to become a concert pianist, your list might include practice every day, play at recitals, memorize music, go to competitions, and study.)

1. _____
2. _____
3. _____
4. _____
5. _____

When I envision myself achieving this goal, I am: (Describe what you are doing and who is with you.)

HABIT **3**

Choose one or two Baby Steps you can do. Share your experiences with someone else, or write your experiences and learnings here.

 Set a goal to use a planner for one month. Stick to your plan.

 Identify your biggest time-wasters. Do you really need to spend two hours on the phone, surf the Web all night, or watch that sitcom rerun?

My biggest time-wasters: _____

_____

 Are you a "pleaser," someone who says yes to everything and every-one? If so, have the courage to say no today when it's the right thing to do.

 If you have an important test in one week, don't procrastinate and wait until the day before to study. Suck it up and study a little each day.

 Think of something you've procrastinated for a long time but that's very important to you. Block out time this week to get it done.

Item I've procrastinated forever:_____

 Note your ten most important Big Rocks for the upcoming week. Now, block out time on your schedule to accomplish each one.

Identify a fear that is holding you back from reaching your goals. Decide right now to jump outside your comfort zone and stop letting that fear get the best of you.

Fear that's holding me back: _____

How much impact does peer pressure have on you? Identify the per-son or people who have the most influence upon you. Ask yourself, "Am I doing what I want to do or what they want me to do?"

Person or people who most influence me: _____

_____

Which of the Baby Steps did I try, and what did I learn?

The Relationship Bank Account

THE STUFF THAT LIFE IS MADE OF

Introduction *E*arlier we spoke of the Personal Bank Account (PBA) and how that represents the amount of trust and confidence you have in yourself. Likewise, the Relationship Bank Account (RBA) represents the amount of trust and confidence you have in each of your relationships with others.

The RBA is just like the checking account at your bank. You can make deposits and improve the relationship, or take withdrawals and deplete the relationship.

So how do you build a healthy and rich RBA? One deposit at a time. The two things that make the RBA slightly different from the PBA is that what may be a deposit to you may not necessarily be a deposit to the other person in the relationship. For example, buying a box of chocolates for someone on a diet may not be a deposit. The other difference is the size of the deposit and that the other person in the relationship determines the withdrawal—not you.

To help you see what I mean, listed below are six deposits and the opposite withdrawals that seem to get the same result every time:

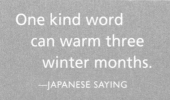

> One kind word
> can warm three
> winter months.
> —JAPANESE SAYING

109

DEPOSIT	WITHDRAWAL
Keep promises	*Break promises*
Do small acts of kindness	*Keep to yourself*
Be loyal	*Gossip and break confidences*
Listen	*Don't listen*
Say you're sorry	*Be arrogant*
Set clear expectations	*Set false expectations*

Some of the most powerful deposits someone has made into my RBA are:

Where am I in my relationships with others? (Write the names of two people and put the dollar amount, either a positive cash balance or in the hole, for each person.)

BALANCE

Name _____ $ _____ + or − _____

Name _____ $ _____ + or − _____

If I were to share this information with those on the list above and ask them if they feel the same way about my RBA balance with them, they would say:

For each category, I could do the following to improve my relationships:

Friends:

Siblings:

Parents or guardian:

Teachers:

Girlfriend or boyfriend:

KEEP PROMISES

The Relationship Bank Account (RBA) chapter teaches that keeping commitments and promises is vital to building trust. You must do what you say you're going to do.

Often, when you don't keep a commitment it's because you probably shouldn't have made it in the first place. Don't say you'll drive a friend to work if you know your parents need the car. Don't promise to babysit for your little sister if you've got a date that night. If you realize you're overcommitted, apologize as soon as possible, and try to find a solution to the problem you've created.

Mend Broken Promises
Read the Keeping Promises section on pages 134–135 of the *Teens* book.

A time when I broke a promise to someone was: (Describe the event.)

I have rebuilt trust with that person now. True or false?

If true, I rebuilt that trust by: (Describe your actions.)

If false, I can rebuild trust by: (Describe your actions.)

A time when someone did not keep a promise to me was: (Describe the event.)

That broken promise made me feel:

Do Small Acts of Kindness

Read the story on page 137 of the *Teens* book, then complete the statements below.

Lee's act of kindness was very simple, yet it yielded great RBA results. A simple act of kindness I could do for other people is:

A time when someone did a simple act of kindness for me was: (Describe that act and how it made you feel.)

A relationship in my life that I would like to improve is:

A simple act of kindness I could do for that person is:

Speed write on a separate piece of paper for a few minutes all the simple acts of kindness you could do today (and for free) for the people you encounter.

• BE LOYAL

In the Relationship Bank Account (RBA) chapter, you learn that being loyal is critical to maintaining healthy relationships. Gossiping and not keeping secrets can do great damage to someone's reputation. When someone asks you to keep a secret, keep it. When someone begins to gossip to you, politely remove yourself from the situation.

Test Your Loyalty

Circle the answer that best describes you:

1. When I hear my friends telling a juicy story about someone I know, I think to myself:
   a. "How do I know that this story is true? I need to give the other person the benefit of the doubt."
   b. "This conversation is making me uncomfortable. I really like the person we're talking about and want to be loyal. I think I should speak up."
   c. "I'm not sure this gossip is true, but I'm really enjoying being part of a group right now. No way am I going to speak up and ruin all that."
   d. "I think I need to leave."

2. When I hear someone stick up for someone I'm gossiping about, I think to myself:
   a. "Oh, lighten up! Everyone enjoys a good drama!"
   b. "I admire that he was able to speak up. I should know better than to talk badly about people."
   c. "He's just jealous he's not the center of attention right now."

3. I feel gossip is:
   a. Just harmless fun—a way of passing time with my friends.
   b. Not fair to those who are not present. I wouldn't want others to gossip about me!
   c. A way of filling up silence when I don't know what to say in a group of people I really want to impress.

4. If someone shares something with me and asks me to keep it "just between you and me," I:
   a. Honor their request and tell no one.
   b. Figure that if they really wanted it to be a secret they wouldn't have told anyone, including me.
   c. Tell only my best friend. But I tell them to keep it a secret too.

5. I feel that gossip causes:
   a. Mistrust. If I hear my friends gossip about others, I wonder if they gossip about me when I'm not around.
   b. A breakdown in loyalty. How can I be a good friend if I don't honor him or her when he or she isn't present?
   c. Lack of confidence. I feel that I can't confide in my friends anymore about my personal problems. What if they can't keep a secret?
   d. No negative effects. Everyone knows it's just gossip—who takes that stuff seriously anyway?

Have you ever heard the saying, "Great minds discuss ideas; small minds discuss people"? Refer to your answers in the questions above. Where are you? Do you feel you have room for improvement? Sometimes groups of people may gossip because it's the easiest thing to talk about. But that doesn't have to be true. Think of an interest you have in common and start a conversation about that! You'll find that your conversations are a lot more worthwhile, and everyone in the group can relax and not worry about hurting others.

LISTEN

In the Relationship Bank Account (RBA) chapter, you learn that listening can be one of the single greatest deposits you can make into another's RBA. Listening to what others are saying shows that you care about them. Listening and caring about those around you forms lasting friendships.

Assess the Listener

Read the Listen section on pages 140–141 of the *Teens* book.

When I am talking to someone, I like it when he or she listens intently and shows these actions:

> You cannot truly listen to anyone and do anything else at the same time.
>
> —DR. M. SCOTT PECK

I can tell if someone is zoning out and not listening to me by: (Describe his or her actions.)

When I am listening to someone else speak, I show him or her that I am listening by: (Describe your actions.)

I feel that listening intently can negatively or positively affect the RBA. True or false?

A time when the RBA between someone else and me was affected was when: (Describe the situation.)

• SAY YOU'RE SORRY

The Relationship Bank Account (RBA) chapter teaches that saying you're sorry when you do something wrong can quickly restore an overdrawn RBA. When you overreact, yell, or make a stupid mistake, the best thing to do is apologize. Everyone makes mistakes, and no one expects you to be perfect. Don't let your pride stand in the way, because it's never as hard as it seems. Admitting mistakes disarms people and can often turn what could have been a disaster into a positive experience. So give it a try and apologize the next time you do something wrong. You'll be amazed at the results.

Practice Apologizing

Read the Say You're Sorry section on pages 141–142 of the *Teens* book.

A time when I apologized for something I did was: (Describe the situation.)

After I apologized, I felt: (Describe your feelings.)

A time when someone apologized to me for something he or she did was: (Describe the situation.)

After he or she apologized, I felt: (Describe your feelings.)

Saying I'm sorry is difficult for me. True or false?

If true, apologizing is difficult because:

> My wife heard me say "I love you" a thousand times, but she never once heard me say "Sorry."
>
> —BRUCE WILLIS

If false, apologizing is easy because:

● SET CLEAR EXPECTATIONS

In the Relationship Bank Account chapter, you learn that by setting clear expectations, you avoid sending vague messages or implying something that is not true or likely to happen. When you start dating someone new, make sure he or she knows that you still want to date other people. When you begin a new job, be sure that your boss understands that you don't want to work late nights. Whenever you get into a new situation or setting, you're better off taking the time to lay all your expectations on the table so that everyone is on the same page. You will build trust with others when you tell it like it is and set clear expectations up front.

Examine Unclear Expectations
Read the Set Clear Expectations section that appears on pages 142–143 of the *Teens* book.

A time in my life when I didn't set clear expectations was: (Describe the event below.)

The results of that situation were:

Choose one or two Baby Steps you can do. Share your experiences with someone else, or write your experiences and learnings here.

Keep Promises

 The next time you go out for the night, tell your mom or dad what time you will be home and keep to it.

 All day today, before giving out any commitments, pause and think about whether or not you can honor them. Don't say, "I'll call tonight," or "Let's have lunch today," unless you can follow through.

Do Small Acts of Kindness

 Buy a burger for a homeless person this week.

 Write a thank-you note to someone you've been wanting to thank for a long time.

Person I need to thank: _____

Be Loyal

 Pinpoint when and where it is most difficult for you to refrain from gossip. Is it with a certain friend, in the locker room, during lunch? Come up with a plan of action to avoid it.

Try to go one whole day saying only positive things about others.

Listen

 Don't talk so much today. Spend the day listening.

Think of a family member you've never really taken the time to listen to, like a little sister, big brother, or grandpa. Take the time.

Say You're Sorry

Before you go to bed tonight, write a simple note of apology to someone you may have offended.

Set Clear Expectations

Think of a situation where you and the other party have different expectations. Put together a plan for how to get on the same page.

Their expectation: _____

_____

My expectation: _____

_____

Which of the Baby Steps did I try, and what did I learn?

HABIT 4

Think Win-Win

Life Is an
All-You-Can-Eat
Buffet

What do we live for if not to make life less difficult for each other?

—GEORGE ELIOT

**Win-Lose—
The Totem Pole**

(H) abit 4: Think Win-Win teaches that Win-Lose is an attitude toward life that says the pie of success is only so big, and if you get a big piece, then someone else will get a small piece. Win-Lose is competitive—relationships, friendships, and loyalty are less important than winning the game, being the best, and having it your way. But in the end, Win-Lose will usually backfire. You may end up on the top of the totem pole, but you'll be there alone and without friends.

People who have a Win-Lose—The Totem Pole attitude usually:

- Use other people, emotionally or physically, for their own selfish purposes.
- Try to get ahead at the expense of others.
- Spread rumors about others.
- Concentrate on getting their own way without considering others' feelings.
- Become jealous and envious when something good happens to someone else.

A situation in which I had a Win-Lose attitude was:

In that situation, I felt:

Change to Win-Win

Read the Win-Lose—The Totem Pole section on pages 147–149 of the *Teens* book.

Look for an article in a newspaper or magazine that shows an example of Win-Lose. Tape that article below:

How could the people in the article have turned their Win-Lose attitude into Win-Win?

What might have been different if both had a Win-Win attitude?

● LOSE-WIN—THE DOORMAT

How is a doormat useful? Pretty much, the only thing it's good for is to wipe your feet on. Its only purpose is to serve others; it doesn't get anything out of the job except being walked all over.

When you think Lose-Win, you essentially become a doormat for other people. Habit 4: Think Win-Win explains that with Lose-Win thinking you'll find yourself setting low or no expectations and compromising your standards again and again. Doesn't sound like fun, does it?

There is a time to lose, of course. Lose-Win is fine if the issue isn't that important to you. Just make sure you stand up for the things you believe in and that matter most.

People with a Lose-Win—The Doormat attitude usually:

- Set low expectations for themselves.
- Have low self-esteem and never consider themselves worthy or good enough.
- Compromise their standards over and over again.
- Give in to peer pressure.
- Allow themselves to be walked on with the excuse of being the "peacemaker."

A situation in which I had a Lose-Win attitude was: (Describe the situation.)

In that situation, I felt:

Change to Win-Win

Read the Lose-Win—The Doormat section on pages 149–151 of the *Teens* book.

I could have changed that situation to Win-Win by: (Describe actions you could have taken.)

● Lose-Lose—The Downward Spiral

Revenge is sweet, isn't it? When someone hurts you, naturally you want to hurt him or her back. It is much easier to seek revenge than to grant forgiveness. However, by getting revenge, you may think you're winning, but you're really hurting only yourself.

Habit 4: Think Win-Win teaches that Lose-Lose is about revenge, winning at all costs, and obsessing about another in a negative way. Lose-Lose says, "If I'm going down, then you're going down with me, sucker."

Lose-Lose is not about winners; it's about losers. You have to decide which team you'd rather be on.

People with a Lose-Lose—The Downward Spiral attitude usually:

- Seek revenge.
- Desire to win at all costs.
- Are obsessed with others in a negative manner.
- Have codependent and emotionally damaging relationships.

A situation in which I had a Lose-Lose attitude was: (Describe the situation.)

In that situation I felt:

● Watch Lose-Lose on TV

Read the Lose-Lose—The Downward Spiral section on pages 151–152 of the *Teens* book.

Watch one of your favorite television shows, then answer the questions below.

What are some Lose-Lose examples you identified in your favorite TV program?

How did Lose-Lose thinking affect the other characters and/or situation?

Was the Lose-Lose thinking turned into Win-Win? Why or why not? And if so, how?

Choose one of your examples of Lose-Lose thinking and explain how it could've been changed into a Win-Win. (If the example was changed into a Win-Win on the show, come up with your own creative Win-Win alternative.)

Avoid Lose-Lose thinking by preparing to Think Win-Win. A specific situation I might face in the next seven days that requires Win-Win thinking is:

Ways I can prepare to Think Win-Win are:

Win-Win—The All-You-Can-Eat Buffet

Think Win-Win is an attitude about life. It's a frame of mind that says I can win, and so can you. It's not me or you; it's both of us. Think Win-Win is the foundation for getting ahead in life by helping others get ahead.

People with a Win-Win attitude usually:
- Are happy when others succeed.
- Help others succeed.
- Think "abundance."
- Are willing to share recognition with others.
- See life as an all-you-can-eat buffet for everybody.

A situation in which I had a Win-Win attitude was: (Describe that situation.)

In that situation I felt:

Apply Win-Win Thinking

Read the Win-Win—The All-You-Can-Eat Buffet section that appears on pages 152–154 of the *Teens* book.

It is hardest for me to Think Win-Win when:

It is easiest for me to Think Win-Win when:

When I practice Win-Win thinking, I enjoy the following benefits:

Five ways I can apply Win-Win thinking in my relationships are:

1. _____
2. _____
3. _____
4. _____
5. _____

WIN THE PRIVATE VICTORY FIRST

Competition is a part of life. In high school, competition is every-where—at sports games, debate competitions, school elections, etc. Competition isn't limited to organized events; you constantly com-pete for grades or attention too. Competition is healthy and promotes a Win-Win attitude when you compete against yourself, or when it challenges you to reach and stretch to become your best.

So how can you Think Win-Win when there's really going to be only one person or team who takes home the prize? Habit 4: Think Win-Win recommends that you start with the Private Victory first.

The Private Victory is about self-mastery and self-discipline. It is about performing your personal best and learning from defeat. Competition becomes dark and spirals into Win-Lose when you tie your self-worth into winning, or when you use it as a way to place yourself above others.

LET'S FIND A **WIN-WIN** SOLUTION, DAD.

Although you might not win every competition, if you can achieve a Private Victory in spite of your loss, you are a winner.

Compete in Style
Read the Win the Private Victory First section on page 154 of the *Teens* book.

The kinds of things I compete in are:

Competition tends to turn ugly for me when:

Select two of the competitive situations you listed above and write them in the table below. Identify how you could win a Private Victory in each situation no matter if you win or lose.

COMPETITION	PRIVATE VICTORY
1.	_____
_____	
2.	_____
_____	

• AVOID THE TUMOR TWINS

In Habit 4: Think Win-Win, you learn to avoid the "tumor twins." Competing and comparing are habits that, like tumors, can slowly eat you away from the inside. It is virtually impossible to Think Win-Win with them around.

In some cases, competition is extremely healthy. It drives you to improve, to reach, and to stretch—to know how far you can push yourself. Competition becomes bad when you tie your self-worth to winning, or when you use it as a way to place yourself above others.

Comparing yourself to others is almost always harmful. You're all on different development timetables—socially, mentally, and physically. Measuring your life based on how you stack up to others is always a bad idea.

Keep Competition Healthy

Read the Avoid the Tumor Twins section on pages 155–158 of the *Teens* book.

Think carefully about your daily activities and see how often you think in terms of comparing and competing. Ask yourself these questions and answer them honestly. Circle the answer that best describes you.

1. If someone gets a better score on a test, I think:
   a) Good for her! She must have made time to study.
   b) Well of course she got a better grade; she has nothing else to do with her time.
   c) I could never get a good grade like that. I'm just not smart enough.

2. While waiting in the checkout line at the grocery store, I review the celebrity magazines in front of me and think:
   a) Wow! They worked hard to get where they are. Good for them.
   b) They only look like that because they have money to pay for trainers, cooks, plastic surgeons, and exercise equipment.
   c) I could never look like that, even with all the money in the world. I'm just not good-looking.

3. At the gym I see some of the local college athletes playing basketball for fun and I think:
   a) I wonder if they'd let me play b-ball with them and learn some new techniques.
   b) They really aren't all that good anyway. I bet Bo-Diddly Tech could whip them with their eyes closed.
   c) They'd never let me play with them. They're way too good and I'm so clumsy.

If you answered "A" to any of the situations, you have successfully avoided the tumor twins, comparing and competing.

If you answered "B" to any of the situations, watch out for an unhealthy competitive attitude. You are thinking Win-Lose or Lose-Win too much.

If you answered "C" to any of the situations, you spend too much time comparing yourself to others. You are in a Lose-Lose situation.

THE FRUITS OF THE WIN-WIN SPIRIT

How do you know if you are thinking Win-Win? Habit 4: Think Win-Win says the true test is how you feel. Win-Lose and Lose-Win thinking cloud your judgment and fill you with negative feelings. On the other hand, thinking Win-Win produces positive and serene thoughts and gives you confidence.

Go for Win-Win

Read The Fruits of the Win-Win Spirit section on pages 159–161 of the *Teens* book.

If you're normal, you're bound to be in an emotional tug-of-war with your parents or in a deadlock with a sibling or friend over a situation that has both of you taking opposite points of view. In the heat of the situation, ask these questions: "How can we come to a Win-Win for both of us? I'm willing to go for Win-Win, are you?"

Do you think your parents will be surprised? How do you think they're going to react?

What will your friends or siblings think or say? Will they distrust you in the beginning? Why or why not?

Draw a picture of their faces or write a creative scenario describing the events and the outcome.

Read about Jacques Lusseyran on page 161 of the *Teens* book. Use your feelings to test whether you Think Win-Win the next time you interact with your family and friends.

Choose one or two Baby Steps you can do. Share your experiences with someone else, or write your experiences and learnings here.

 1. Pinpoint the area of your life where you most struggle with comparisons. Perhaps it's with clothes, physical features, friends, or talents.

Where I'm struggling most with comparisons: _____

_____

 2. If you play sports, show sportsmanship. Compliment someone from the opposing team after the match or game.

 3. If someone owes you money, don't be afraid to mention it in a friendly way. "Did you forget about that ten bucks I loaned you last week? I could use it right now." Think Win-Win, not Lose-Win.

4. Without caring whether you win or lose, play a card, board, or computer game with others just for the fun of it.

5. Do you have an important test coming up soon? If so, form a study group and share your best ideas with each other. You'll all do better.

 6. The next time someone close to you succeeds, be genuinely happy for them instead of feeling threatened.

7. Think about your general attitude toward life. Is it based on Win-Lose, Lose-Win, Lose-Lose, or Win-Win thinking? How is that attitude affecting you?

8. Think of a person who you feel is a model of Win-Win. What is it about this person you admire?

Person: _____

What I admire about them: _____

_____

 9. Are you in a Lose-Win relationship with a member of the opposite sex? If you are, then decide what must happen to make it a Win for you or choose to go for No Deal and get out of the relationship.

Which of the Baby Steps did I try, and what did I learn?

HABIT 5

Seek **First** to
Understand,
Then to Be Understood

**You Have
Two Ears**
AND ONE MOUTH . . .
Hel-lo!

The deepest need of the human heart is to be understood.

—STEPHEN R. COVEY

The Deepest Need of the Human Heart

What if you went to the doctor and he or she prescribed some medication without diagnosing your illness? Would you be sure that the medication would cure you? Would you trust the doctor and follow his or her orders?

Habit 5: Seek First to Understand, Then to Be Understood explains the importance of diagnosing before prescribing. In communication, this works as you listen first and talk second.

This habit makes communication work, since the deepest need of the human heart is to be understood. Everyone wants to be respected and valued for who and what he or she is—an individual. Think of the saying, "People don't care how much you know until they know how much you care." How do you feel when someone doesn't take the time to really listen to you? It feels as if they don't really care.

THESE SHOULD HELP YOU FEEL BETTER.

BUT I HAVE A STOMACHACHE.

Search Your Feelings

Read The Deepest Need of the Human Heart section that appears on pages 165–167 of the *Teens* book.

Two or three things I wish my parents understood about me are:

1. _____

2. _____

3. _____

Two or three things I wish my teachers understood about me are:

1. _____

2. _____

3. _____

Two or three things I wish my friends understood about me are:

1. _____

2. _____

3. _____

Two or three things I wish my brothers or sisters understood about me are:

1. _____

2. _____

3. _____

Someone I know who is struggling with a problem is:

How can I make him or her feel comfortable, accepted, and understood around me?

FIVE POOR LISTENING STYLES

You can't understand someone who's talking if you don't listen carefully. Surprise! Like most of us, you probably don't know how to listen well. We are too busy preparing a response, judging, or making their words fit our own paradigms. Typically, we use one of these five poor listening styles:

1. Spacing out: Someone is talking to you, but you ignore him or her because your mind is elsewhere.

A time when someone spaced out while listening to me was:

It made me feel:

I find myself doing this to someone often. True or false?

If true, when? And who is that person?

2. Pretend listening: You're not paying attention to the person talking, but you pretend you are. When you think the person wants a response, you say, "Uh-huh, cool, yeah, hmmm."

A time when someone used pretend listening while listening to me was:

It made me feel:

I find myself doing this to someone often. True or false?

If true, when? And who is that person?

3. Selective listening: You pay attention only to the part of the conversation that interests you or relates to you. You key in on specific words and then go off on your own conversation rather than listening to what the other person is trying to tell you.

A time when someone used selective listening while listening to me was:

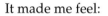

It made me feel:

I find myself doing this to someone often. True or false?

If true, when? And who is that person?

4. Word listening: You pay attention to the words, but you miss the point because you're ignoring the tone, feelings, and body language. When you focus on words only, you miss the deeper emotions in someone's heart.

A time when someone used word listening while listening to me was:

It made me feel:

I find myself doing this to someone often. True or false?

If true, when? And who is that person?

5. Self-centered listening: You apply everything you hear to your own point of view. You say, "Oh, I know just what you mean," or "I know exactly how you feel." Well, you don't know exactly how he or she feels, and you haven't listened long enough to show you even care. This is where some people play the one-upmanship game: "If you think your day was bad, wait until I tell you about mine!"

A time when someone used self-centered listening while listening to me was:

It made me feel:

I find myself doing this to someone often. True or false?

If true, when? And who is that person?

Go to a busy place, such as a mall or school, where you'll see lots of people talking to each other. For twenty minutes, observe people talking to each other. Write a scenario of what you think was going on or being said.

Observation 1   *Where:*
_____

                        Scenario:
_____

_____

_____

_____

                        Was good listening happening? Yes or No
_____

Observation 2   *Where:*
_____

                       Scenario:
_____

_____

_____

_____

                       Was good listening happening? Yes or No
_____

● GENUINE LISTENING

How often do you find yourself using one of the five poor
listening styles instead of genuinely listening
to another person? Are you even hearing
what they are trying to say?

Habit 5: Seek First to Understand, Then
to Be Understood explains that genuine listening
involves:

- Listening with your eyes, heart, and ears.
- Standing in the other person's shoes.
- Mirroring (using your own words to reflect the
  other person's feelings).

Make sure you use these techniques only when you're talking about
an important or sensitive issue. If you use these techniques during
casual conversation or everyday small talk, people might think you
are weird or insincere.

● IDENTIFY GENUINE OR POOR LISTENING

1. Read the Genuine Listening section on pages 171–176 of the
   Teens book.
2. Read the following four scenarios and answer the questions
   for each.

Scenario 1

Ellie flopped onto her bed and stared at the ceiling. Maren, her sister, looked up from her book and asked, "Rough day?"

"Something like that," was all Ellie said before settling back into silence. She sighed.

Maren waited a minute before she spoke. "Do you want to talk about something?"

"No."

"Okay." Maren turned back to her book.

Ellie continued to lie on the bed, saying nothing. Every now and then, she would sigh in disgust. "Boys are stupid, you know?" she finally spit out.

"Yeah, they are," Maren agreed as she closed her book.

"I don't know why I even bother with them. Guess what Rick told me today?"

"What?" asked Maren.

Was this an example of genuine listening or poor listening? Why?

If poor listening was demonstrated, how could the scenario be changed to show genuine listening?

HABIT 5

Scenario 2

Kim answered the phone. "Hello?"

"Hey, there," her friend Maria said. "I have got to talk to you."

"What's up?"

"Well, remember that dress we saw at the mall—the spaghetti-strap blue one with the low back?" Maria asked.

"I think so. Wasn't it in the same store where I tried on that really sexy pink thing? I should've bought it. Mike would've gone crazy when he saw me in it. You want to go to the mall?"

"Uh, not right now," Maria replied. "But anyway, so that blue dress was on sale the other day—"

"On sale!" Kim exclaimed. "Well, then we've definitely gotta go over there today. Maybe the pink dress is on sale too."

"I can't go today. I have dance class," Maria responded, exasperated.

"Oh, come on. You can skip class for this. I mean, you want that dress, right? Of course you do! So, we're going to the mall today. I can't let you pass this dress up. You looked great in it."

"I'm glad you think so, because my mom—"

Beep.

"Hey, can you hold on a sec? I've got another call."

When Kim clicked over, Maria was finally able to say, "So, my mom bought me the dress as a surprise." And then she hung up.

Was this an example of genuine listening or poor listening? Why?

If poor listening was demonstrated, how could the scenario be changed to show genuine listening?

Scenario 3

Christian looked up and down the hallway. He was new to the school and wasn't sure where his next class was. The bell rang, letting Christian know that wherever it was, he was going to be late for it.

"Hey man," a male voice called out. "Are you lost or just ditching?"

Christian turned around toward the voice to see a guy who looked about his age. "Lost, unfortunately," Christian replied. "This school is much bigger than my old one."

"So, what you're saying is that this is a big school and you feel lost in it."

Christian looked at him, confused. "It is a big school, and I literally am lost. Do you know where room 319 is?"

"You feel confused and alone."

Was this guy for real? Christian thought. "You're making me confused by trying to analyze my feelings. I'm supposed to be in room 319 for my English class, and I don't know where it is. So, if you know where it is, I'd appreciate your help. If not, I'll just find it on my own."

The guy looked at him quizzically and then said, "I can see that you're frustrated."

"Ugh!" Christian sighed and walked off.

Was this an example of genuine listening or poor listening? Why?

If poor listening was demonstrated, how could the scenario be changed to show genuine listening?

Scenario 4

Tyrone's little sister, Lana, was starting to get on his nerves. She was always following him around, trying to hang out with him and his friends when they came over after school. After she had spent most of the afternoon showing his friends her soccer trophies and trying to get them to go in-line skating with her, he had had enough.

"Lana, why can't you just leave me and my friends alone? Can't you see we don't want to hang with you?"

Lana looked up at him, and he could see the hurt in her eyes. "You don't want me around?"

"No," Tyrone replied, and looked away from her.

Her voice quivering, Lana said, "Okay. I'm sorry. You guys are the coolest. I didn't mean to bug you."

She thinks I'm cool, Tyrone thought with a mixture of guilt and pride. I guess that's why she's always hanging around. It must be weird for her now that I'm always off with my friends and don't see her as much.

"Lana, I'm sorry. I shouldn't have yelled at you. I like to hang out with my friends by myself now and then, but we can get together and do something this week—just you and me."

"You mean it?" Lana smiled. "That would be great."

Was this an example of genuine listening or poor listening? Why?

If poor listening was demonstrated, how could the scenario be changed to show genuine listening?

GENUINE LISTENING—FIRST, LISTEN WITH YOUR EYES, HEART, AND EARS

Habit 5: Seek First to Understand, Then to Be Understood teaches that if you want to understand what other people are really saying, you need to listen to what they don't say. How can you hear something that isn't said?

Try listening with your eyes, heart, and ears. Don't just pay attention to the words people say; watch their body language, hear their tone, and sense how they are feeling.

Hear More Than Words

Read the Listen with Your Eyes, Heart, and Ears section that appears on pages 171–172 of the *Teens* book.

At home, at the mall, or in the halls at school, watch for body language. Describe the different forms of body language and what they mean to you.

FORM OF BODY LANGUAGE	WHAT IT MEANS

GENUINE LISTENING—SECOND, STAND IN THEIR SHOES

Habit 5: Seek First to Understand, Then to Be Understood teaches that if you want to understand someone else, try looking at things from his or her perspective. Be willing to stand in someone else's shoes to see things from a different point of view.

Diagnose a Parent

1. Read the Stand in Their Shoes subsection on pages 172–173 of the *Teens* book.
2. Imagine that you are a reporter for a local television station.
3. Using the questions provided, conduct an interview with a parent or teacher.

Take notes during the interview, and write his or her
responses in the space provided.

Name of parent or teacher: _____

1. If you could buy one thing for yourself, and money was no object,
   what would it be and why?

2. If you could change one thing about yourself, what would it be?

3. What is your favorite movie and why?

4. What is your most precious memory?

5. What thing do you fear the most?

6. What's the one thing that always makes you happy?

7. What's the one decision you'd change if you were given a second chance?

8. When was the last time you laughed so hard it hurt?

● LISTENING—THIRD, PRACTICE MIRRORING

Have you ever talked to someone who responded but who you knew wasn't really listening to you?

In Habit 5: Seek First to Understand, Then to Be Understood, you learn that genuine listening involves responding in a way that helps the speaker feel understood. This type of response is called mirroring. Mirroring means to repeat back in your own words what the other person is saying.

If you use mirroring but don't really want to understand others, they will see through you and feel manipulated. Mirroring is a skill—the tip of the iceberg. Your attitude or desire to really understand another is the lurking mass of ice underneath the surface.

Decide When to Use Mirroring
Read the Practice Mirroring subsection on pages 173–175 of the *Teens* book.

If someone said the following phrases to you, what is a mirroring phrase you could reply with? Write your answers below.

"This is the worst paper I've ever read!"
Mirroring Phrase:

"You absolutely cannot stay out past midnight."
Mirroring Phrase:

"I don't know that new girl very well."
Mirroring Phrase:

"My parents are really driving me nuts lately."
Mirroring Phrase:

HABIT 5

"Lunch was really good today."
Mirroring Phrase:

"I don't feel like going to work."
Mirroring Phrase:

COMMUNICATING WITH PARENTS

I bet you've said to your parents, "You don't understand me!" Have you ever stopped to consider that perhaps you don't understand them?

Habit 5: Seek First to Understand, Then to Be Understood points

out that your parents have pressures and worries just like you do. They have days when they get offended, when they cry, and when people laugh at them. They wonder if they fit in and if they will achieve their goals—just like you do.

If you take time to understand and listen to your parents, you will gain more respect for them, and they will be more likely to trust and listen to you.

One way to communicate better with your parents is by making deposits in their Relationship Bank Accounts (RBAs). You can make deposits and improve the relationship, or take withdrawals and weaken it. Your relationship is strong and healthy when you make steady deposits over a long period of time.

Make sure you identify what a deposit is to the person whose RBA you are trying to improve.

Agree on Deposits and Withdrawals

1. Read the Communicating with Parents section that appears on pages 176–178 of the *Teens* book.
2. Try to remember everything you did for a parent or family member yesterday. List things that your parent or family member would consider to be deposits or withdrawals.

Parent   *Family Member*

_____   _____

_____   _____

_____   _____

WITHDRAWALS

Parent   *Family Member*

_____   _____

_____   _____

_____   _____

SEEK TO BE UNDERSTOOD

The first half of Habit 5 requires a lot of work, so many people forget the second half of Habit 5, "Then to Be Understood." Seeking first to understand someone else requires that you show consideration. Seeking then to be understood requires courage. Practicing just the first half of this habit is Lose-Win, and Lose-Win is not healthy.

Unexpressed feelings never die—they are buried alive and just come forth later in uglier ways. That sounds really scary doesn't it? So what other things are you afraid of?

If you asked a hundred people what their greatest fears were, speaking in public would be number one, and death would be number two. Can you believe that? People would rather die than speak in public! Are you one of them?

Giving Feedback

Giving feedback to someone who is talking to you is an important part of seeking to be understood. If it's done right it can be a deposit into your PBA and into someone else's RBA.

Do you have a situation in your life right now where you need to give feedback but are afraid to? What is that situation? And who is it with?

Come up with three possible ways to give feedback so it isn't frightening for you and isn't threatening to the other person.

Person: _____

1. _____

2. _____

3. _____

Practice all three possible ways you can give someone feedback. When one seems to be authentic and sincere, go give it a shot!

BABY STEPS

Choose one or two Baby Steps you can do. Share your experiences with someone else, or write your experiences and learnings here.

 See how long you can keep eye contact with someone while they are talking to you.

 Go to the mall, find a seat, and watch people communicate with each other. Observe what their body language is saying.

 In your interactions today, try mirroring one person and mimicking another, just for fun. Compare the results.

 Ask yourself, "Which of the five poor listening styles do I have the biggest problem with – Spacing Out, Pretend Listening, Selective Listening, Word Listening, or Self-Centered Listening (judging, advising, probing)? Now, try to go one day without doing it.

The poor listening style I struggle with most:_____

_____

 Sometime this week, ask your mom or dad, "How's it going?" Open up your heart and practice genuine listening. You'll be surprised by what you learn.

 If you're a talker, take a break and spend your day listening. Only talk when you have to.

7 The next time you find yourself wanting to bury your feelings deep inside you, don't do it. Instead, express them in a responsible way.

8 Think of a situation where your constructive feedback would really help another person. Share it with them when the time is right.

Person who could benefit from my feedback: _____

_____

Which of the Baby Steps did I try, and what did I learn?

HABIT 6

Synergize

1+1= 3

The
"High" Way

Alone we can do so little; together we can do so much.
—HELEN KELLER

Synergy Is Everywhere

(S)ynergy happens when two or more people work together to create a better solution than one of those people could come up with alone. It's not your way or my way, but a better way, a higher way. Synergy isn't anything new; it's everywhere.

Check out this list of what synergy is and is not:

SYNERGY IS . . .	SYNERGY IS NOT . . .
Keeping promises	*Breaking promises*
Being happy that we're different	*Just tolerating differences*
Working in teams	*Working alone*
Being open-minded	*Thinking you're always right*
Thinking outside the box	*Always coloring within the lines*
Coming up with Third Alternatives	*Compromising*
Brainstorming	*Insisting on only one right answer*

Let's look at synergy in people. How many people do you think it takes to build a car? Could one person do it alone? No. It takes creative cooperation to design, build, and sell cars. People work together using their unique expertise. Their differences spark ideas and help the company create innovative solutions.

Observe Synergy

Read the Synergy Is Everywhere section on page 183 of the *Teens* book.

The places I see synergy around me are: (Give examples of synergy for each category.)

Nature:

School:

Family:

Community or church:

Work:

6 HABIT

● **CELEBRATING DIFFERENCES**

Diversity is a tough topic among teens. During my teenage years I was trying to blend in, not be different. But without diversity, life would be extremely boring. If everyone thought like you, looked like you, and acted like you, you could get a little sick of yourself.

When you hear the word diversity, you typically think of racial and gender differ-ences. But it also means differences in phys-

ical features, dress, language, wealth, family, religious beliefs, lifestyle, education, interests, skills, age, style, and on and on.

Habit 6: Synergize teaches that since diversity is inevitable, you can take three possible approaches:

Level 1: Shun diversity

Level 2: Tolerate diversity

Level 3: Celebrate diversity

When you celebrate diversity, you want to cooperate with others to achieve your goal.

Find Your Approach to Diversity

Read the Celebrating Differences section on pages 183–185 of the *Teens* book.

The things I can do to become a celebrator in each category are:

Race:

Gender:

Religion:

Age:

Dress:

Body type:

Abilities/Disabilities:

● RESPECT DIFFERING VIEWPOINTS

Habit 6: Synergize defines synergy as people who work together to achieve more (1 + 1 = 3 or more). It's much easier to work with others when you appreciate their differences. Once you understand that everyone views the world differently and that everyone can be right, you have more respect for differing viewpoints.

> I once complained to my father that I didn't seem to be able to do things the same way other people did. Dad's advice? "Margo, don't be a sheep. People hate sheep. They eat sheep."
>
> —MARGO KAUFMAN

● RANK YOUR CHARACTER TRAITS

Assess your styles, traits, and characteristics by completing the table on the next page. Look at the four terms in each row and rank them from 1 to 4, with 4 next to the word that best describes you. (See the legend box on the next page.) After you have completed the table, ask a friend or family member to complete a table too. Then total the columns in both surveys.

Legend

4—Best describes you (you are exactly like this).

3—Mostly describes you (you are kind of like this).

2—Hardly describes you (you're not really like this).

1—Least describes you (you are nothing like this).

Example

Imaginative	2	Investigative	4	Realistic	1	Analytical	3

COLUMN 1		COLUMN 2		COLUMN 3		COLUMN 4	
Imaginative		Investigative		Realistic		Analytical	
Adaptable		Inquisitive		Organized		Critical	
Relating		Creating		Getting to point		Debating	
Personal		Adventurous		Practical		Academic	
Flexible		Inventive		Precise		Systematic	
Sharing		Independent		Orderly		Sensible	
Cooperative		Competitive		Perfectionistic		Logical	
Sensitive		Risk-taking		Hard-working		Intellectual	
People-person		Problem solver		Planner		Reader	
Associate		Originate		Memorize		Think through	
Spontaneous		Changer		Wants direction		Judger	
Communicating		Discovering		Cautious		Reasoning	
Caring		Challenging		Practicing		Examining	
Feeling		Experimenting		Doing		Thinking	
COLUMN 1 TOTAL		**COLUMN 2 TOTAL**		**COLUMN 3 TOTAL**		**COLUMN 4 TOTAL**	

COLUMN 1		COLUMN 2		COLUMN 3		COLUMN 4	
Imaginative		Investigative		Realistic		Analytical	
Adaptable		Inquisitive		Organized		Critical	
Relating		Creating		Getting to point		Debating	
Personal		Adventurous		Practical		Academic	
Flexible		Inventive		Precise		Systematic	
Sharing		Independent		Orderly		Sensible	
Cooperative		Competitive		Perfectionistic		Logical	
Sensitive		Risk-taking		Hard-working		Intellectual	
People-person		Problem solver		Planner		Reader	
Associate		Originate		Memorize		Think through	
Spontaneous		Changer		Wants direction		Judger	
Communicating		Discovering		Cautious		Reasoning	
Caring		Challenging		Practicing		Examining	
Feeling		Experimenting		Doing		Thinking	
COLUMN 1 TOTAL		**COLUMN 2 TOTAL**		**COLUMN 3 TOTAL**		**COLUMN 4 TOTAL**	

After completing both tables, and totaling all columns, refer to pages 187 to 189 in the *Teens* book. Determine what fruit you both are. Now, think about how you can capitalize on your differences and work together more synergistically.

> Greetings. I am pleased to see that we are different. May we together become greater than the sum of both of us.
>
> —MR. SPOCK

- ## WE ARE ALL A MINORITY OF ONE

Because each person is unique, you are truly a minority of one. No one person looks, talks, or even thinks the same as you do. Habit 6: Synergize reminds you that diversity isn't just an external thing. It's also internal. You learn differently; you see differently; and you have different styles, traits, and characteristics. Your brain doesn't work the same as your sister's or your friend's.

Dr. Thomas Armstrong identified seven kinds of intelligence and said that young people may learn best through their most dominant intelligence:

- Linguistic: Learn through reading, writing, and telling stories.
- Logical/Mathematical: Learn through logic, patterns, categories, and relationships.
- Bodily/Kinesthetic: Learn through bodily sensations and touching.
- Spatial: Learn through images and pictures.
- Musical: Learn through sound and rhythm.
- Interpersonal: Learn through interaction and communication with others.
- Intrapersonal: Learn through their own feelings.

One of these learning types is not better than another, only different. Synergy is learning to see the advantages in the differences.

Examine Learning Types and Natural Abilities

Read the We Are All a Minority of One section on pages 186–189 of the *Teens* book.

Of the dominant intelligences listed above, I feel that my dominant intelligence is:

Other dominant intelligences I use are: (Also describe when and where.)

(Refer back to the survey you just completed on page 160. Then see pages 187–189 of the *Teens* book.) The fruit I most resemble is:

(Read the natural abilities of each fruit on pages 188–189 of the *Teens* book.) I feel that the list of natural abilities for my fruit describes me pretty well. True or false?

Of the natural abilities on the list, I feel that my strongest natural ability is:

A time when that natural ability came in handy was: (Describe the situation.)

NOTICE THE DIFFERENCES

Do you know what it means to be a minority of one? No one else is in this minority with you, not even if they look similar to you or have the same background as you. Even if you had an identical twin, you would still be a minority of one. Once you look beyond the surface, you will find amazing differences that make everyone unique.

DISCOVER YOUR DIFFERENCES

Refer to the We Are All a Minority of One section on pages 186–189 of the *Teens* book.

Fill out the following survey to help you discover what is great and unique about you!

> The smallest minority on earth is the individual.
>
> —AYN RAND

1. A nickname my friends or family call me is:

   _____

2. My hometown is:

   _____

3. When I have a day all to myself, I love to:

   _____

4. The movie I laughed the hardest at was:

   _____

5. At night, how many pillows do I use?

   _____

6. A word or phrase I use all the time is:

   _____

7. My favorite musical artist or group is:

   _____

8. My favorite ice cream is:

   _____

9. My typical bedtime is:

   _____

10. One quality that makes me unique is:

    _____

11. My best friend would say that my best quality is:

    _____

12. My best subject in school is:

    _____

13. My worst subject in school is:

    _____

14. The animal that is most like me is: (Why?)

    _____

15. If I could own any car in the world, it would be:

    _____

16. My best feature is:

    _____

17. Do I feel more comfortable in a large group of people or by myself?

    _____

18. One thing people don't know about me is:

_____

19. When I daydream, I think about:

_____

20. My best family memory is:

_____

21. Would spending a day in an art museum be fun or boring for me?

_____

22. If I could visit any city in the United States, it would be: (Why?)

_____

23. If I could visit any country in the world, it would be: (Why?)

_____

24. The best vacation I ever took was:

_____

25. The worst vacation I ever took was:

_____

26. If I could be any building in the world, I would be: (Why?)

_____

27. Something that keeps me awake at night is:

_____

28. Something I enjoyed doing as a child was:

_____

29. My favorite sport to watch is:

_____

30. My favorite book is:

_____

31. The season I love the most is:

_____

32. My favorite holiday is:

_____

33. The silliest person I know is:

_____

34. Do I prefer the indoors or outdoors?

_____

35. The best present I could ever receive is:

_____

CELEBRATE YOUR OWN DIVERSITY

Comparing yourself to others is easy. After all, you see other people more than you see yourself. However, when you compare yourself to another person, you neglect to recognize the beauty of your uniqueness.

Habit 6: Synergize teaches that instead of trying to blend in and be like everyone else, you should be proud of and celebrate your unique differences and qualities. A fruit salad is delicious precisely because each fruit maintains its own flavor.

Appreciate Your Uniqueness

Read the Celebrate Your Own Diversity section on pages 189–190 of the *Teens* book.

The fruits I would include in my fruit salad are:

The fruits I would leave out are:

The next time I compare myself to someone else and feel I come up short, I will appreciate my own uniqueness by remembering which one of my strengths?

Instead of trying to blend in and be like everyone else, I will be proud of and celebrate my unique differences and qualities by:

• AVOID ROADBLOCKS TO CELEBRATING DIFFERENCES

Although celebrating differences has many roadblocks, three of the largest are:

- Ignorance: Not knowing how other people think, what they believe, or how they feel.
- Cliques: Wanting to be with those you're comfortable with, which isn't wrong, but it becomes a problem when that group becomes exclusive and rejects others.
- Prejudice: Not treating people fairly, which includes stereotyping, labeling, or prejudging others because they differ from your own circumstances.

These roadblocks are the opposite of celebrating differences and, therefore, prevent synergy from occurring.

Identify Diversity Roadblocks

A time when I suffered because of someone's ignorance or saw someone else suffer for the same reason was:

A time when I was outside a clique or observed someone else outside a clique was:

> Fear makes strangers
> of people who
> should be friends.
>
> —SHIRLEY MACLAINE

Something I can do to avoid treating others with prejudice is:

An area in which I might be prejudiced is:

One thing I can do to overcome this prejudice is:

STICK UP FOR DIVERSITY

What would the world be like if no one ever stuck up for diversity? Instead of being in color, the world would probably be more black-and-white. It would be a very unfriendly and uneducated place where no one would be willing to share his or her differences. The absence of diversity would become very monotonous.

Habit 6: Synergize explains that, fortunately, the world is full of people who value diversity. These people celebrate differences and are willing to stick up for diversity. The knowledge and understanding that come from differences of opinion, race, cultures, and lifestyles are invaluable.

However, you can't simply rely on others to stick up for diversity. You have to be willing to stand up for it yourself.

> Differences create the challenges in life that open the door to discovery.—American Sign Language for "we are diverse"

Discover How to Stick Up for Diversity

Sticking up for diversity is important to me. True or false? (Why?)

A time when I stuck up for diversity (or could have) is:

What happened?

For one day, observe the people around you, the TV shows and movies you watch, and the books you read. Keep a "Sticking Up for Diversity Journal" below. Record the examples you can find of sticking up for diversity.

TYPE OF DIVERSITY	HOW SOMEONE STUCK UP FOR DIVERSITY
_____	_____
_____	_____
_____	_____
_____	_____

I was surprised by how many examples of sticking up for diversity I found. True or false? Did you expect to find more or less?

I can overcome my fears about sticking up for diversity by: (Describe your thoughts or actions.)

Answer the following questions true or false. Think about specific instances in your life before answering.

❑ True ❑ False I demand perfection from myself and everyone around me.

❑ True ❑ False I am surprised when others don't like me or my ideas.

❑ True ❑ False People continually make promises to me without following through.

❑ True ❑ False I don't have many friends whom I really like or trust.

❑ True ❑ False I get tired of all this "political correctness." I don't have to like everyone.

❑ True ❑ False I don't appreciate other people's opinions of me.

❑ True ❑ False I don't like change.

❑ True ❑ False I work better alone than in groups.

❑ True ❑ False I tend to be more negative than positive.

❑ True ❑ False I'm afraid people will find out that I'm not what I appear.

If the majority of your answers are "true," it's time to start understanding the lives and actions of others. Appreciate what everyone can bring to the party. If the majority of your answers are "false," you're comfortable with yourself and how you relate to people of all kinds. You know that learning from others helps you in your life.

FINDING THE "HIGH" WAY

Habit 6: Synergize explains that once you've bought in to the idea that differences are a strength and not a weakness, and you've committed to celebrate differences, you're ready to find the High Way—synergy. It's not your way or my way, but a better way—a higher way.

The Founding Fathers found the High Way as they formed the structure of the U.S. government. William Paterson proposed the New Jersey Plan that favored the smaller states. James Madison offered the Virginia Plan that favored the larger states. The result? The Connecticut Compromise, often called the Great Compromise, formed two chambers of Congress—the House and Senate—and satisfied the desires of both the smaller and larger states. However, it should be called the Great Synergy, since it proved to be better than either of the original proposals.

Go for Something Higher

Read the Finding the "High" Way section on pages 193–195 of the *Teens* book. Synergy is more than just compromise or cooperation; it's finding a Third Alternative that helps everyone involved like the outcome.

A time when I merely compromised with someone else was:

I was unhappy with the outcome. True or false?

HABIT 6

We could have reached a High Way by:

A time when I reached a High Way with someone else was:

After reaching the High Way, I felt:

How I think the other person felt:

GETTING TO SYNERGY

What if you are arguing with your parents over dating and curfew guidelines, or planning a school activity with your peers and simply not seeing eye to eye? You can still get to synergy.

In Habit 6: Synergize, you learn that you can achieve synergy using a simple five-step process.

Use the Getting to Synergy Action Plan

Read the Getting to Synergy section that appears on pages 195–200 of the *Teens* book.

Getting to Synergy
ACTION PLAN

? **DEFINE THE PROBLEM
OR OPPORTUNITY**

THEIR WAY
(Seek first to understand the ideas of others.)

MY WAY
(Seek to be understood by sharing your ideas.)

BRAINSTORM
(Create new options and ideas.)

HIGH WAY
(Find the best solution.)

PHOTOCOPY THIS ACTION PLAN AND PLACE IT WHERE YOU CAN REFER TO IT OFTEN.

Identify one relationship you would like to improve. Use the Getting to Synergy Action Plan to resolve your differences and/or achieve synergy.

One relationship I would like to improve is:

The problem or opportunity is:

How I can seek first to understand the ideas of the other person is:

How I can seek to be understood by sharing my ideas is:

New options and ideas I could consider are:

The best solution we found was:

● TEAMWORK AND SYNERGY

The wonderful by-product of teamwork and synergy is a good relationship. Basketball Olympian Deborah Miller Palmore said it well: "Even when you've played the game of your life, it's the feeling of teamwork that you'll remember. You'll forget the plays, the shots, and the scores, but you'll never forget your teammates."

Some people are better at synergizing than others. They find joy in supporting, uplifting, and sustaining others to create a better outcome than what could be done alone. Achieving synergy is a gift anyone can develop! Anytime you work with people to make a better outcome, you are getting synergy.

Decide Who You Can Count On

Read the Teamwork and Synergy section on pages 200–201 of the *Teens* book.

Write the names of friends, teachers, family members, or others who best fit the descriptions below:

I can count on _____ to help me with homework.

I can count on _____ for a good meal that lifts my day.

I can count on _____ to answer my questions about life in general.

I can count on _____ to help plan an activity or a party.

I can count on _____ to know my deepest thoughts and help me with them.

I can count on _____ to keep a secret.

I can count on _____ to come up with the best music for a dance.

I can count on _____ to help me clean the yard or house.

I can count on _____ to play ball with me.

I can count on _____ to shop with me and give me good ideas.

I can count on _____ to teach me math.

I can count on _____ to help me plan my education.

I can count on _____ when I have spiritual or religious questions.

I can count on _____ to always love me and build me up.

Others can count on my synergy in these areas:

> A mouse does not rely on just one hole.
> —PLAUTUS

Choose one or two Baby Steps you can do. Share your experiences with someone else, or write your experiences and learnings here.

 When you meet a classmate or neighbor with a disability or impairment, don't feel sorry for them or avoid them because you don't know what to say. Instead, go out of your way to get acquainted.

 The next time you are having a disagreement with a parent, try out the Getting to Synergy Action Plan. 1. Define the problem. 2. Listen to them. 3. Share your views. 4. Brainstorm. 5. Find the best solution.

 Share a personal problem with an adult you trust. See if the exchanging of viewpoints leads to new insights and ideas about your problem.

④ This week, look around and notice how much synergy is going on all around you, such as two hands working together, teamwork, symbiotic relationships in nature, and creative problem solving.

⑤ Think about someone who irritates you. What is different about them?

What can you learn from them? _____

_____

 Brainstorm with your friends and come up with something fun, new, and different to do this weekend, instead of doing the same old thing again and again.

 Rate your openness to diversity in each of the following categories. Are you a shunner, tolerator, or celebrator?

	SHUNNER	TOLERATOR	CELEBRATOR
Race			
Gender			
Religion			
Age			
Dress			

What can you do to become a celebrator in each category?

_____

Which of the Baby Steps did I try, and what did I learn?

The time to repair the roof is when the sun is shining.
—JOHN F. KENNEDY

Introduction H abit 7: Sharpen the Saw is about balanced renewal in all four dimensions of human need: physical, mental, social/emotional, and spiritual. As you renew yourself in each of the four areas, you create growth and change in your life. You increase your capacity to produce and handle the challenges around you. When you don't renew yourself, you limit or even reverse your growth, and limit or decrease your capacity to produce and your ability to handle challenges.

So you're thinking "I don't have time to Sharpen the Saw." How can sharpening the saw increase capacity? Think about it:
- Time to cut a log with a dull saw—thirty minutes
- Time to sharpen the saw—five minutes
- Time to cut the log with a sharp saw—ten minutes

Ka-ching! You just saved yourself fifteen minutes. You've never cut a log? How does this apply to you?
- Time left until your deadline and you're exhausted—five hours
- Time to Sharpen the Saw, refocus, and feel ready to go—thirty minutes
- Time to finish the project when you're refreshed—three hours

Ka-ching! You just saved yourself ninety minutes. That's how it applies to you.

Rate How You Renew
1. Read the Sharpen the Saw introduction section on page 206 of the Teens book.
2. Complete the assessment below and on the next page.

N = Never   S = Sometimes   A = Always

	N	S	A
I eat a nutritious diet and try to stay away from junk food.	N	S	A
I exercise regularly.	N	S	A
I get enough sleep.	N	S	A

	N	S	A
I take care of personal hygiene.			
I take time to relax.			

	N	S	A
I regularly read good books, magazines, or newspapers, or I listen to the news.			
I play or listen to good music.			
I write or draw.			
I attend cultural events, watch uplifting movies, or view educational television programs.			
I learn new skills and develop my talents.			

	N	S	A
I laugh out loud at least once a day.			
I make deposits into my Relationship Bank Accounts.			
I make deposits into my Personal Bank Account.			
I use my talents.			
I develop new relationships.			

	N	S	A
I pray or meditate regularly.			
I keep a journal.			
I read poetry or other inspiring literature.			
I ponder my decisions and situations in life.			
I enjoy nature by going on walks, looking at landscapes, or taking time to enjoy a sunset.			

3. In thirty days, take the assessment again. Fill in your answers with a different colored pen. Compare your responses with those from the first assessment you completed.

The differences between the two assessments are:

- ## BALANCE IS BETTER

Habit 7: Sharpen the Saw is about keeping your personal self sharp so you can better deal with life. To perform at your peak, you need to pay attention to all four dimensions. Balancing them is important because what you do in one dimension of life will affect the other three. Think about it. If one of your car's tires is out of balance, all four tires will wear unevenly, not just one. It's hard to be friendly (heart) when you're exhausted (body). It also works the other way. When you're feeling motivated and in tune with yourself (soul), it's easier to focus on your studies (mind) and be more friendly (heart).

Maintain Your Balance

1. Read the Balance Is Better section that appears on page 207 of the *Teens* book.
2. In the table below, list three ways you renew yourself in each dimension.

DIMENSION	HOW I RENEW MYSELF		
Body	_____	_____	_____
Brain	_____	_____	_____
Heart	_____	_____	_____
Soul	_____	_____	_____

> Everyone is a house with four rooms: physical, mental, emotional, spiritual. Unless we go into every room every day, even if only to keep it aired, we are not a complete person.
> —RUMER GODDEN

3. Identify new ways to renew yourself.

DIMENSION	HOW I CAN RENEW MYSELF		
Body	_____	_____	_____
Brain	_____	_____	_____
Heart	_____	_____	_____
Soul	_____	_____	_____

Take Time for a Time-Out

Habit 7: Sharpen the Saw teaches that, like a car, you need regular tune-ups and oil changes. You need time to rejuvenate and rest. You need time to relax and unstring your bow. Treat yourself to a little pampering—that is what sharpening the saw is all about.

Find Ways to Relax

Read the Take Time for a Time-Out section that appears on page 207 of the *Teens* book.

> Within you is a stillness and sanctuary to which you can retreat at any time and be yourself.
>
> —HERMANN HESSE

Ten things I can do to take a time-out are:

1. _____
2. _____
3. _____
4. _____
5. _____
6. _____
7. _____
8. _____
9. _____
10. _____

> People who cannot find time for recreation are obliged sooner or later to find time for illness.
>
> —JOHN WANAMAKER

Ways I have seen others relax in the past month are:

● **CARE FOR YOUR BODY**

During your teenage years, your voice will change, your hormones will run rampant, and curves and muscles will begin springing up all over. Welcome to your new body!

Habit 7: Sharpen the Saw explains that this ever-changing body of yours is really quite a marvelous machine. You can handle it with care, or you can abuse it. You can control it, or let it control you. In short, your body is a tool, and if you take good care of it, it will serve you well.

Assess Your Physical Renewal

Read the Caring for Your Body section on pages 208–215 of the *Teens* book.

Assess your physical wellness by placing a checkmark next to the items that you do regularly.

❑ I stay informed and current on both health and fitness information.

❑ I exercise twenty to thirty minutes at least three times a week.

❑ I am fully aware of my need for fruits, vegetables, vitamins, and minerals.

❑ I increase or maintain a strength program.

❑ I include cardiovascular and flexibility activities in my exercises.

❑ I get the right amount of sleep.

❑ I rest or relax when my body needs it.

❑ I eat junk food or fast food less than twice a week.

❑ I deal with stress effectively and positively.

To me, health and renewal means:

> Your body will honor
> you with wellness
> if you honor it
> with awareness.
>
> —ANONYMOUS

An activity that I've seen other people doing that I'd like to try is:

I want to learn more about nutrition. True or false? Specifically, I am
interested in:

I want to learn more about fitness. True or false? Specifically, I am interested in:

To achieve physical health, you might need to go beyond your usual
idea of what health and fitness really are. If you're struggling to feel
your best, refer to the checklist on page 184. Would
one of the unchecked items be a good place to start?

• EXAMINE WHAT YOU EAT

Part of Habit 7: Sharpen the Saw is paying attention
to your health. You can't do anything without it. So for
peak performance, you need the right fuel.

What are you eating?

To avoid extremes in your diet, use the USDA
food pyramid as a guide. The food pyramid is a
moderate and balanced approach to nutrition. It encourages you to eat more whole grains, fruits, vegetables, and low-fat
dairy products and to avoid fast food, junk food, and snacks, which
are often loaded with fat, sugar, and salt.

The old saying "everything in moderation" applies to food and other parts of life.

Fats, Oils, and Sweets (USE SPARINGLY)

Milk, Yogurt, and Cheese Group (2–3 SERVINGS)

Meat, Poultry, Fish, Dry Beans, Eggs, and Nuts Group (2–3 SERVINGS)

Vegetable Group (3–5 SERVINGS)

Fruit Group (2–4 SERVINGS)

Bread, Cereal, Rice, and Pasta Group (6–11 SERVINGS)

USDA FOOD PYRAMID *(Balanced)*

Track What You Eat

Listen to your body—pay attention to how different foods make you feel. From that knowledge, develop your own do's and don'ts. Everybody responds differently. For example, if some people eat a big meal before bed, they don't sleep well and feel terrible in the morning.

Use the following food diary form to track what you eat for one week.

Su _____

M _____

T _____

W _____

Th _____

F _____

Sa _____

Can you see a link between what you ate and how you felt?

(Answer this at the end of the week.) I was surprised to see how well or how poorly I ate. True or false? (Describe your feelings below.)

The areas I see for improvement in my diet are:

How much you exercise can also affect the way you feel. For one week, use the exercise diary form below to track how many minutes a day you exercise.

	Minutes	*Activity*
Su		
M		
T		
W		
Th		
F		
Sa		

● FOCUS ON HOW YOU FEEL, NOT ON HOW YOU LOOK

In your quest for a better physique, make sure you don't get too obsessed with your appearance. As you've probably noticed, society is hung up on "looks." Just walk into any grocery store and look at the perfect people who are on the covers of nearly every magazine. Kind of makes you feel self-conscious about your physical imperfections, doesn't it?

Before you start comparing yourself to the models on the covers of *Cosmopolitan* and *Muscle and Fitness* and begin hating everything about your body and looks, remember that thousands of healthy and happy teens don't have high cheekbones or rock-hard abs. In fact, many successful singers, talk show hosts, dancers, athletes, actors, and actresses have all kinds of physical imperfections but are still admired and successful.

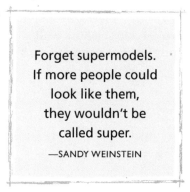

Forget supermodels. If more people could look like them, they wouldn't be called super.

—SANDY WEINSTEIN

The important thing is feeling good physically—not so much looking good physically.

Paste Up Great Personalities

If you believe everything that magazine covers tell you, you might think that you have to be thin, glamorous, chiseled, and toned to be admired or popular. Not true! To prove this point, go through magazines and clip pictures of three celebrities who are just "everyday people" and who are healthy physically.

Paste the pictures on the next page.

To get started, look at this list of celebrities—they are admired, popular, and successful because they are talented, have an endearing personality, are funny, or have their own type of beauty:

- John Goodman (voted one of the "sexiest men alive" by *People* magazine)
- Harrison Ford (popular because he's thought of as a regular-looking "everyman")
- Bruce Willis and Woody Harrelson (both have receding hairlines)
- Janeane Garofalo (popular because of her personality and humor)

Choose one person from the pictures pasted on the previous page. Who is the person and what trait do you think makes this person popular?

How do I feel about myself?

Are these feelings healthy or unhealthy? Why do you think that?

If unhealthy, how can I change that perception?

AVOID DESTRUCTIVE ADDICTIONS

Just as there are ways to care for your body, there are ways to destroy it. And using addictive substances such as alcohol, drugs, and tobacco is the fastest way to do it. Alcohol, for example, is often associated with the three leading causes of death among teens: car accidents, suicide, and homicide. As well as being a major cause of lung cancer and respiratory disease, smoking has been proven to cloud your eyes, cause premature skin aging, yellow your teeth, triple your cavities, cause receding gums, and discolor your skin.

Perhaps the worst thing about picking up an addiction is you're no longer in control—your addiction is. You may think addiction is something that happens to someone else and that you could quit anytime. In reality, it's hard. Only 25 percent of teen tobacco users who try to quit are successful.

The destructive addictions I would like to change are:

A place I will go for help is: (See page 249 in the *Teens* book for a list of resources.)

Test Your Alcohol Smarts

Let's see how much you know about alcohol and its dangers. Answer the following true or false. Check your answers after you have completed the test.

1. ❑ True ❑ False   Most teens are drinking alcohol.

2. ❑ True ❑ False   Beer and wine are "safer" than liquor.

3. ❑ True ❑ False   As long as you're not drinking, being around others who are won't hurt anything.

4. ❑ True ❑ False   You can't overdose on alcohol.

5. ❑ True ❑ False   Alcohol damages your body.

6. ❑ True ❑ False   Alcohol damages your brain.

7. ❑ True ❑ False   Drinking alcohol makes you more attractive.

8. ❑ True ❑ False   You can't say no to alcohol and still fit in.

9. ❑ True ❑ False   Drinking alcohol is something you do on the weekend; it doesn't affect school performance.

10. ❑ True ❑ False   It is illegal to buy or possess alcohol if you are under twenty-one years old.

11. ❑ True ❑ False   All teenagers will drink at some point, no matter what.

12. ❑ True ❑ False   The following are slang names for alcohol: booze, sauce, brews, brewskis, hooch, hard stuff, juice.

13. ❑ True ❑ False   It doesn't matter if you mix alcohol with other drugs—like medicine.

Answer Key

1. False. The vast majority of teens do not drink.
2. False. One can of beer has about as much alcohol as a glass of wine, a wine cooler, or a shot of liquor.
3. False. If you're around people who are drinking, you have an increased risk of being seriously injured, involved in a car crash, or affected by violence.
4. False. Drinking large amounts of alcohol can lead to coma or even death.
5. True. Alcohol can damage every organ in your body. It goes directly into your bloodstream and can increase your risk for a variety of serious diseases.
6. True. Drinking alcohol slows your brain and your central nervous system, and leads to a loss of coordination, poor judgment, slowed reflexes, distorted vision, memory lapses, and even blackouts.
7. False. Alcohol can make you gain weight and give you bad breath.
8. False. Remember, you're in good company. The majority of teens don't drink alcohol. Also, it's not as hard to refuse as you might think. Try "No thanks," "I don't drink," or "I'm not interested."
9. False. High school students who use alcohol or other addictive substances are five times more likely than other students to drop out of school or to believe that earning good grades is not important.
10. True.
11. False. Although underage drinking is a serious problem, 84 percent of people aged twelve to seventeen have chosen not to drink in the past month.
12. True.
13. False. Mixing alcohol with medicine or other drugs is extremely dangerous and can lead to accidental death.

Information from the U.S. Department of Health and Human Services.

CARE FOR YOUR BRAIN

The mental dimension of Habit 7: Sharpen the Saw means developing brain power through your schooling, extracurricular activities, hobbies, jobs, and other mind-enlarging experiences.

An educated mind is much more than a diploma on a wall, even though that's an important part of it. An educated mind is like a well-conditioned ballerina. A ballerina has perfect control over her muscles. Her body will bend, twist, jump, and turn perfectly at her command. Similarly, an educated mind can focus, synthesize, write, speak, create, analyze, explore, imagine, and so much more. To do that, however, takes training. It doesn't just happen.

In today's world, if you don't keep yourself mentally sharp, you're in big trouble. Mental stimulation comes from a wide variety of sources—fiction, art, educational TV, puzzles, and games can be about stretching yourself mentally as well.

Assess Your Brain Power

1. Read the Caring for Your Brain section that appears on pages 216–227 of the *Teens* book.
2. Complete the following assessment:

N = Never   S = Sometimes   A = Always

	N	S	A
I read newspapers daily.	N	S	A
I keep a journal or some sort of log, or have a regular writing time.	N	S	A
I travel to see different cultures or areas of historical interest.	N	S	A
I enjoy watching the Discovery Channel, the Learning Channel, or PBS.	N	S	A
I listen to or watch the news on radio, TV, or the Internet daily.	N	S	A
I set aside some time for silence to clear my mind, relax, and think about things.	N	S	A

HABIT 7

	N	S	A
I have researched my family roots.			
I have written a poem, song, or story.			
I play challenging card or board games.			
I have been on the debate team.			
I visit museums.			
I go to cultural events such as plays, ballets, operas, or the symphony.			
I can play a musical instrument.			
I like to do crossword puzzles.			
I have deep and stimulating conversations with friends.			
I use the Internet to research topics for school.			
I know how to use a computer.			
I can follow a recipe and cook a good meal.			
I know at least a little about car maintenance and repair.			
I have a library card.			
I do a good job on my homework.			
I have made plans to continue my education.			
I have taken a foreign language in school.			
I read books just for fun.			

3. Give yourself three points for each check in the "Always" column, two points for "Sometimes," and one point for "Never."

    > 55 points and over—You are a brainiac!
    > 41–55—Your brain is getting a fair amount of work
    > Under 40 points—You need to pay more attention to your mental development.

4. In ninety days, take the assessment again. Fill in your answers with a different colored pen. Compare your scores with those from the first assessment you completed.

The differences between the two assessments are:

> Take out your brain and jump on it— it gets all caked up.
>
> —MARK TWAIN

SHARPEN YOUR MIND

You can find a million ways to keep your mind alert and sharp. But quite simply, the easiest and quickest way is to read. Just simply read. Reading is the foundation for everything else. But if you're already doing that, here are some more ways to sharpen your mind.

* Read a newspaper every day (local paper, school paper, or *USA Today*).
* Go to class, stay awake, and take notes.
* Watch PBS occasionally.
* Get involved in local politics.

Keep Sharp
I keep my mind sharp by:

> Keep learning about the world. Use your mind to the hilt. Life passes quickly and, toward the end, gathers speed like a freight train running downhill. The more you know, the more you enrich yourself and others.
>
> —SUSAN TROTT

This week I learned these things that I didn't know before:

My favorite book is:

The last book I read to someone else was: (And when?)

Remember what you learned in the Paradigms and Principles chapter about becoming too school-centered? Well, keep that in mind when caring for your mind. Of course, you don't want to drop out of school! Grades are important because they lead to future educational opportunities. But you can get other educational opportunities from school, not just grades.

Don't get too worried or stressed today about your college major. If you can simply learn to think well and are well rounded in your activities, you will have plenty of career and education options to choose from.

Future careers I feel an interest in pursuing are:

What I am doing now to determine if that's really what I want to do is:

• CARE FOR YOUR HEART

Do you ever feel as if you're riding an emotional roller coaster—up one day and down the next? Your heart is temperamental. And it needs constant nourishment and care, just like your body.

Habit 7: Sharpen the Saw teaches that the best way to nourish your heart is to nourish relationships—both with yourself and with others. Over time, good feelings build on one another. If you approach life this way, you'll be amazed at how much happiness you can give others and find for yourself.

Meaningful relationships are not like the mold accumulating on the cheddar cheese in your fridge. They require conscious effort. Don't forget, each relationship is like a bank account. The quality of the relationship depends on what you put into it.

Strengthen a Relationship

Maintaining strong relationships with others is a vital part of caring for your heart. But just as you learned in the Paradigms and Principles chapter about becoming too friend-centered, you are more likely to ride an emotional roller coaster if you let your friends influence how you feel about yourself.

> The most important ingredient we put into any relationship is not what we say or what we do, but what we are.
>
> —STEPHEN R. COVEY

The relationship in my life that I can strengthen is:

The benefits that would come from building others up instead of tearing them down are:

Check off the items that describe you:

❑ I am reliable and dependable.

❑ I have a hopeful outlook on life.

❑ I am trusting and supportive of people who are close to me.

❑ I listen to others and hear what they have to say rather than thinking of what I want to say next.

❑ I reach out to others.

❑ I maintain my most important relationships.

❑ I sincerely apologize when I need to.

❑ I can push through the "hard times."

❑ I am aware of what it means to take good care of myself.

❑ I can control my impulses. I cool down rather than react to people and situations.

If you're struggling to "care for your heart," refer to the checklist above. Would one of the unchecked items be a good place to start?

● EXAMINE SEX AND RELATIONSHIPS

Habit 7: Sharpen the Saw encourages you to care for your heart by developing your closest relationships. One of the closest relationships you have could be with a boyfriend or girlfriend. In these relationships, intimacy becomes a decision that many teens have to face.

Sex is about a whole lot more than your body. It's also about your heart. In fact, what you do about sex may affect your self-image and your relationships with others more than any decision you make. So, before you decide to have sex or to continue having it, you better think about it, real hard.

Investigate Your Readiness

Think you're ready to go all the way? Are you sure? Sexually transmitted infections, an unplanned pregnancy, and emotional doubts are all good reasons to wait! Before you go too far, take a look at this list and check off the items that describe you.

You're not ready to have sex if:

❑ You think sex equals love.

❑ You feel pressured.

❑ You're afraid to say no.

❑ It's just easier to give in.

❑ You think everyone else is doing it. (They're not.)

❑ Your instincts tell you not to.

❑ You don't know the facts about pregnancy.

❑ You don't understand how birth control works.

❑ It goes against your moral beliefs.

❑ You don't think a woman can get pregnant the first time. (She can.)

❑ It goes against your religious beliefs.

❑ You'll regret it in the morning.

❑ You feel embarrassed or ashamed.

❑ You're doing it to prove something.

❑ You can't support a child.

❑ You can't support yourself.

❑ Your idea of commitment is a three-day video rental.

❑ You believe sex before marriage is wrong.

❑ You don't know how to protect yourself from HIV—the virus that causes AIDS.

❑ You don't know the signs and symptoms of sexually transmitted infections (STIs, also called STDs).

❑ You think it will make your partner love you.

❑ You think it will make you love your partner.

❑ You think it will keep you together.

❑ You hope it will change your life.

❑ You don't want it to change your life.

❑ You're not ready for the relationship to change.

❑ You're drunk.

❑ You wish you were drunk.

❑ Your partner is drunk.

❑ You expect it to be perfect.

❑ You'll just die if it's not perfect.

❑ You can't laugh together about awkward elbows and clumsy clothes.

❑ You're not ready to take off your clothes.

❑ You think HIV and AIDS only happen to other people.

❑ You think you can tell who has HIV by looking at them.

❑ You don't think teens get HIV. (They do.)

❑ You don't know that abstinence is the only 100-percent protection against sexually transmitted infections and pregnancy.

❑ You haven't talked about tomorrow.

❑ You can't face the thought of tomorrow.

❑ You'd be horrified if your parents found out.

❑ You're doing it just so your parents will find out.

❑ You're too scared to think clearly.

❑ You think it will make you more popular.

❑ You think you "owe it" to your partner.

❑ You think it's not OK to be a virgin.

❑ You're thinking only about yourself.

❑ You're not thinking about yourself.

❑ You can't wait to tell everyone about it.

❑ You hope no one will hear about it.

❑ You really wish the whole thing had never come up.

❑ It's OK to wait.

Excerpted from You're Not Ready to Have Sex If. . . . *Copyright 1996 Journeyworks Publishing, Santa Cruz, Calif. Reprinted with permission.*

Something I learned about myself from the list was: (Describe why it was useful.)

Making the wrong decision about having sex can affect my future and relationships because:

My decision about sex will affect my self-image and my relationships with others in these ways:

Test your partner's resolve. If you are pressured to have sex, ask your partner what would happen if you refused. If your partner says, "I will break up with you," then it's probably a good idea to break up the relationship.

● KNOW YOU'RE GONNA MAKE IT

Life has a way of piling up and making you feel as if you're ready to lose your mind. When you feel down, discouraged, or overwhelmed, try these pickups:

- Get some oxygen. Focused breathing can help you control your physical responses to stress. Put your tongue on the roof of your mouth behind your teeth, inhale deeply through your nose, and fill up with air until your stomach sticks out. Then slowly release the air through your nose or mouth. Do this at least three times. It will help you loosen up and settle down.
- Take a perspective check. Ask yourself, "Will I care about this in a month? In a year?" If you're going to freak out, make sure it's for a good reason. If your reason for stressing out suddenly seems ridiculous, laugh it off.
- Choose your response. Pick the appropriate and productive emotion: anger, courage, humor, compassion, sadness, or whatever. Any emotion is okay as long as you remain in control and handle the situation with a little grace.

It's totally normal to feel depressed sometimes. But sustained depression is extremely different.

If you are having thoughts of suicide, please hold on for dear life. You're gonna make it. Depression is treatable. If the person you talk to isn't hearing what you're saying, please talk to or call somebody who can help. There are people who really care about you.

Fight Depression Like Crazy

I find myself feeling down in these instances:

It lasts (how long?):

I pull myself out of it by: (Describe your actions.)

I have someone I can talk to. True or false?

That person is:

He or she listens to me by: (How does he or she listen?)

He or she is easy to talk to because:

● **LAUGH OR YOU'LL CRY**

After all is said and done, there is one key ingredient to keeping your heart healthy and strong. Just laugh, loud and long and clear. (Isn't that what Mary Poppins said?)

> Life loves to be taken by the lapel and told, "I'm with you, kid. Let's go."
>
> —MAYA ANGELOU

Did you know that by the time you reach kindergarten, you laugh about three hundred times a day? In contrast, the typical adult laughs a measly seventeen times a day. Where are you? Three hundred times a day or seventeen?

Laughter also promotes good health and speedy recoveries, so it's not just good for your heart—it's good for your body!

If you're not laughing much now, do something about it. Start a humor collection—collect funny stories, funny movies, and jokes. Remember to never let your laughter become unkind or at the expense of others. Learn to laugh at yourself when strange things happen to you or when you do something kind of stupid.

Look for Ways to Laugh

These things always make me laugh:

My three favorite funny movies are:

1. _____

2. _____

3. _____

My favorite line from a movie that just cracks me up is:

My favorite comic strip in the newspaper is:

My favorite comedian/comedienne is:

Something that made me laugh today was:

> **Laughter is the shortest distance between two people.**
>
> —VICTOR BORGE

Care for Your Soul

Your soul is your center. In your soul lies your deepest convictions and values. It is the source for purpose, meaning, and inner peace. Habit 7: Sharpen the Saw teaches that sharpening the saw in the spiritual area of life means taking time to renew and awaken that inner self.

THAT'S IT! WE'RE SWITCHING TO NICKELODEON.

What would happen to someone who drank only soft drinks and ate only chocolate for several years? What would he or she look like and feel like after a while? Would the result be any different if you fed your soul trash for several years? You're not only what you eat, you're also what you listen to, read, and see. More important than what goes into your body is what goes into your soul.

Your soul is a very private area of your life. You can feed it in many ways. Here are some ideas shared by others:

- Meditating
- Listening to inspirational music
- Serving others
- Praying
- Being in nature

Feed Your Soul the Good Stuff

I feed my soul by: (Describe your actions.)

Some new things I would like to add are:

HABIT 7

Am I feeding my soul nutrients or junk? Am I putting things into my soul that I really don't want in there? Some of these things are:

You choose what you're going to feed your soul with—don't let the world decide for you. The media has a light side and a dark side.

The kind of media I am exposing my soul to is:

The media exposure that I find harmful to my moods is:

I think this happens because:

Rate Your Ability to Care for Your Soul

Check off the items that describe you:

❑ I have defined what my values are and I plan to live my life accordingly.

❑ I have created my mission statement. I rely on it to give vision to my purpose in life.

❑ I renew each day through meditation, prayer, study, or reflection.

❑ I frequently spend time in a place where I can spiritually renew, such as in nature, a synagogue, a chapel, or a temple.

❑ I live with integrity and honor.

❑ I keep my heart open to the truth.

❑ I make a stand or tell the truth, even when opposed by others.

❑ I frequently serve others with no expectations of a returned favor.

❑ I can identify which things in life I can change and which things I cannot. I let go of the things I cannot change.

GETTING BACK TO NATURE

Habit 7: Sharpen the Saw explains that there is something magical about getting into nature. Even if you live in a downtown area far removed from rivers, mountains, or beaches, there is usually a park nearby. Getting into nature is a great way to nourish your soul.

> The soul was never put in the body to stand still.
>
> —JOHN WEBSTER

Make a Date with Nature

1. Read the Getting Back to Nature section that appears on page 235 of the *Teens* book.
2. Choose one of these activities to help you get in touch with nature this week:
   - Plant some flowers, vegetables, or herbs.
   - Weed a flower bed or vegetable garden every day this week.
   - Mow or water the lawn once this week.
   - Watch the sunset and sunrise and notice their differences.
   - Look on your calendar to see the date of the next full moon. Schedule time to look at it.
   - Watch for the different phases of the moon, and recognize how each phase affects the way the moon looks.
   - Take a walk in your neighborhood. Notice the types of trees you see, the birds that fly there, the insects that crawl around, and the flowers that grow.
   - Go to the zoo. Choose two different animals to observe, and watch them for fifteen minutes each. Identify the differences between them.
   - Compare a river to a lake. Recognize the differences between them.

HABIT 7

- Identify different states of water (for example, ice, clouds, etc.). Find examples of these in your community.
- Go to the hills or mountains near you, and identify natural habitats.

The activity I chose was: _____

My experience with nature made me feel: (Describe your experience.)

GET REAL

When you think about renewal do you think, "Get real. Who has the time? I'm at school all day, I have activities after school, and I study all night." There is a time for everything—a time to be balanced and a time to be imbalanced. Imbalance happens, and you will have times when you don't get enough sleep, eat too much junk food, and spend too much time studying or working to get any exercise. But there are also times for renewal.

If you go too hard for too long, you won't think as clearly, you'll be cranky, and you'll begin to lose perspective. You think you don't have time for building relationships, getting exercise, spending time getting in touch with your soul; but in reality, you don't have time not to.

> Balance is the key to success in all things. Do not neglect your mind, body, or spirit. Invest time and energy in all of them equally—it will be the best investment you ever make, not just for your life but for whatever is to follow.
>
> —TANYA WHEWAY

Regain Your Balance

I have been out of balance lately. True or false?

Why or why not?

I can get back into a more stable and balanced routine by doing:

Believe it or not, just doing this workbook is helping you create more balance in life—if you've done the exercises and the Baby Steps, if you've taken time to feed your body, your mind, your heart, and your soul! Good job!

Choose one or two Baby Steps you can do. Share your experiences with someone else, or write your experiences and learnings here.

Body

 1. Eat breakfast.

2. Start an exercise program today and do it faithfully for 30 days. Walk, run, swim, bike, rollerblade, lift weights, etc. Choose something you really enjoy.

3. Give up a bad habit for a week. Go without alcohol, soda pop, fried foods, donuts, chocolate, or whatever else may be hurting your body. A week later, see how you feel.

Mind

 4. Subscribe to a magazine that has some educational value, such as *Popular Mechanics* or *National Geographic.*

5. Read a newspaper every day. Pay special attention to the headline stories and the opinions page.

6. The next time you go on a date, visit a museum or eat at an ethnic restaurant you've never been to before. Expand your horizons.

Heart

7. Go on a one-on-one outing with a family member like your mom or your brother. Catch a ball game, see a movie, go shopping, or get an ice cream.

8. Begin today to build your humor collection. Cut out your favorite cartoons, buy hilarious movies, or start your own collection of great jokes. In no time, you'll have something to go to when you're feeling stressed.

Soul

 9. Watch the sunset tonight or get up early to watch the sunrise.

 10. If you haven't already done it, start keeping a journal today.

11. Take time each day to meditate, reflect upon your life, or pray. Do what works for you.

Which of the Baby Steps did I try, and what did I learn?

BABY STEPS

LEARNINGS JOURNAL

Keep Hope Alive!

KID, YOU'LL MOVE MOUNTAINS!

Keep Hope Alive

(T) his workbook was written to help you through the difficult and tumultuous teenage years—to help you navigate through the jungle and give you hope to succeed! The hope is that you can move forward, kick an addiction, get out of an abusive relationship, establish lifelong habits of effectiveness, get organized, and lead a balanced life. That's not asking much, is it?

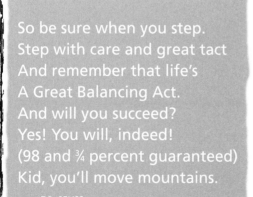

If after reading *The 7 Habits of Highly Effective Teens* and after completing this personal workbook you are feeling overwhelmed and don't know where to start, try doing some Baby Steps.

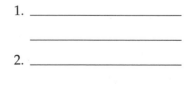

Thumb back through this personal workbook and ask yourself, "Which one or two habits am I having the *most* difficult time living?"

Then choose just one or two things to work on. Write them down here.

1. _____
   _____

2. _____
   _____

So be sure when you step.
Step with care and great tact
And remember that life's
A Great Balancing Act.
And will you succeed?
Yes! You will, indeed!
(98 and ¾ percent guaranteed)
Kid, you'll move mountains.

DR. SEUSS,
FROM *OH, THE PLACES YOU'LL GO*

3. _____

Start on those habits and you'll be amazed at the
results you'll see in yourself after a few small changes.
You're gonna feel more confident and happier—you'll experience a natural high. When you have that success,
move on to the next.

The best way to internalize any of these habits is
to share them with someone else while they're fresh
on your mind.

I will share these ideas with the following person:

If you ever find yourself getting discouraged or falling short, remember that small adjustments have huge returns. Keep your hope
alive!

Go for the best—you deserve it! And don't forget this great quote
in the *Teens* book:

> You can't make footprints in the sands of time by sitting on your
> butt. And who wants to leave buttprints in the sands of time?
>
> —BOB MOAWAD

Write your own closing quote to a workbook just completed—and a
journey just beginning:

Choose one or two Baby Steps you can do. Share your experiences with someone else or write your experiences and learnings here.

 I will keep a journal of my innermost feelings, dreams, aspirations, and goals.

I will review this workbook and ask myself how I feel about the answers I gave. I will carefully review my life: Am I where I want to be, or am I on the right path to get to where I want to be?

I will memorize a quote that will help inspire me when I get discouraged.

I will keep hope alive! And I will help others keep hope alive, too.

Which of the Baby Steps did I try, and what did I learn?

About FranklinCovey

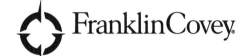 FranklinCovey.

FranklinCovey is a global leader in effectiveness training, productivity tools, and assessment services for organizations and individuals. Our clients include 90 percent of the Fortune 100, more than 75 percent of the Fortune 500, thousands of small and midsize businesses, and numerous government and educational institutions.

Organizations and individuals access FranklinCovey products and services through corporate training, certified client facilitators, one-on-one coaching, public workshops, catalogs, over 180 retail stores, and www.franklincovey.com.

FranklinCovey's purpose is to help organizations succeed by unleashing the power of their workforce to focus on and execute their top priorities. We do this through a series of assessments, work sessions, and tools designed to get everyone focused on the few "wildly important" goals that, if achieved, make all the difference.

Our core products and services include:

- xQ Survey and Debrief: This tool helps leaders assess their organization's "execution quotient."
- Workshops: Our corporate and public workshops include Aligning Goals for Results, FOCUS: Achieving Your Highest Priorities, The 7 Habits of Highly Effective People, and The 4 Roles of Leadership.
- Planning Systems: In addition to the Franklin Planner, we also offer these Planning Systems: Tablet Planner for the Tablet PC, PlanPlus for Microsoft Outlook, FranklinCovey Planning Software, Palm OS, and Pocket PC Software.

STUDENTS AND EDUCATORS
PRAISE THE 7 HABITS TEENS CURRICULUM

Measurable Results from 7 Habits Teens Training
Character Development Student Survey 2000–2001

■ second week   ▨ eighteenth week

Statement	second week	eighteenth week
I feel in control of my life.	3.57	4.53
I care about the well-being of others.	4.00	4.06
I exercise my mind by reading, learning, etc.	3.64	3.73
People say I am a good listener.	3.85	4.00
I set goals regularly.	3.42	3.66
I am happy for my friends when they do well.	4.35	4.60
Other people often have valuable ideas.	3.78	4.13
I begin each day by planning.	2.78	3.20
I keep my promises.	3.85	4.33
I prioritize my work and do most important things first.	3.35	3.86
I communicate well.	3.64	4.20
I exercise regularly and eat healthy foods.	3.07	3.66
I am organized.	3.07	3.86
I enjoy working with others on projects.	2.64	3.60

Results: Joilet Township High School, Joilet, IL. Reprinted with permission.

"The 7 Habits of Highly Effective Teens Workshop is a most powerful experience for children. I've watched them change . . . immediately. They *got* the Habits. It's been one of the most exciting programs I've been involved with!"

Patricia Rogers-Caroselli, Asst. Principal, Ingraham High School

"Teaching us how to organize our daily schedules and how to balance the stress from day-to-day workloads was a very powerful experience. Learning the basics of the 7 Habits . . . was an enlightening experience for all."

Cristal Campbell-Allin, student, Lord Beaverbrook High School, Calgary, Alberta

WORKSHOP OPTIONS

To certify,
call 1-800-272-6839, or visit
www.7Habits4Teens.com

One-Day Workshop

In the one-day workshop, students will learn the time-tested principles of the 7 Habits and how to apply them to the tough issues and life-changing decisions they face. This workshop is full of fun, relevant, and interactive exercises. They'll laugh while they learn with a newfound belief in their own abilities. In addition to the book *The 7 Habits of Highly Effective Teens*, each participant will also receive the Success Guide workbook (36 pages).

Included for facilitators is a PowerPoint presentation, overhead transparencies, and cool videos designed just for teens. This workshop can also be adapted to teach the use of an agenda or a planner.

In-Depth Course

This program allows teens to delve deeper into each of the habits and to truly apply them to their lives. Each teen participant will receive the book *The 7 Habits of Highly Effective Teens* as well as the Ultimate Activity Guide workbook (276 pages), which contains more than 200 individual and group activities focused around the major themes and applications of the 7 Habits.

The materials for this in-depth course were designed to provide optimum flexibility for facilitators and educators. They can be used to teach a semester-long course; direct a self-paced learning course; supplement existing lesson plans; reinforce current-event topics; or hold a church, school, community, or work-related retreat or seminar.

TO BECOME A CERTIFIED 7 HABITS TEENS FACILITATOR . . .

Call 1-800-272-6839 or visit www.7Habits4Teens.com today if you are interested in facilitating this training program, which has been proven to help youth become prepared to stand up for themselves and resist peer pressure, be more goal-oriented, and view life as a positive, meaningful experience.

Upon completion of certification you will receive a facilitator kit, which includes:

- The *7 Habits of Highly Effective Teens* **book**
- **Program video (multiple video clips)**
- **PowerPoint CD, overhead transparencies (17 set), and audio CD**
- **Two Facilitator Guides (One-Day and Ultimate Activity Guide)**
- **Two Teen Participant Guidebooks (Success Guide and Ultimate Activity Guidebook)**
- *Ultimate Activity Guide Facilitator* **video**
- **Activity materials**

SEND IN YOUR STORY!

Hi. Sean Covey here.
Everyone loves a good story. They teach powerful lessons, help us avoid making stupid mistakes, and are just plain fun to read.

So I want to know your story.

Do you have a story of how the 7 Habits helped you overcome a challenge in your life either at school, work, or home? Did any one of the 7 Habits make a difference in your life?

Did you find a new friend, resist peer pressure, or achieve a new goal because of the influence of the 7 Habits? If so, I'd love to hear about it. Please write it up, include all the juicy details, and send it by letter or e-mail.

I'm looking for great stories to include in a future book, and if I decide to use your story, you could win a *free* Palm*. Happy writing!

Send your story to:

FranklinCovey
The 7 Habits for Teens
Attn: Sean Covey
2200 West Parkway Boulevard
Salt Lake City, UT 84119-2331

E-mail: sean.covey@franklincovey.com
Web site: www.7Habits4Teens.com

* Palm Pilot or substitute model of personal digital assistant to be determined at time of award.

Sean Covey was born in Belfast, Ireland, and currently lives in Alpine, Utah, with his wife, Rebecca, and their children. He works for FranklinCovey as vice president of innovation and product development. He graduated with honors from BYU with a degree in English and later earned his M.B.A. from Harvard Business School. As the starting quarterback for BYU, he led his team to two bowl games and was twice selected as the ESPN Player of the Game. He is a popular speaker to youth and adult groups.

Sean's favorite activities include going to movies, working out, designing products, teaching, riding his dirt bike, hanging out with his family, eating Mexican food, sleeping, and writing stupid poetry.

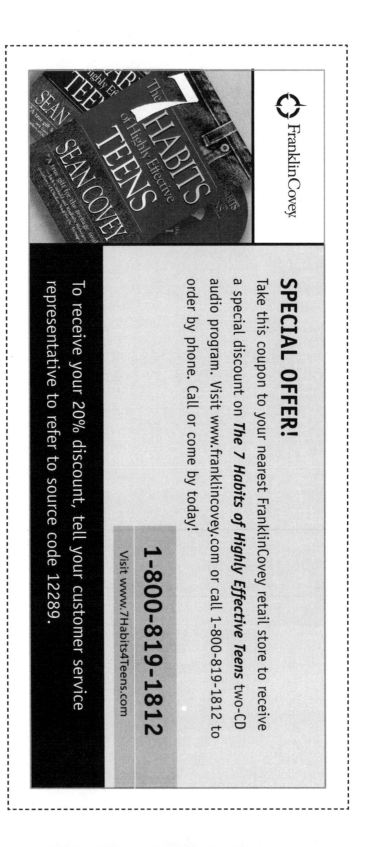

This publication is a personal workbook and is intended exclusively for individual use. This work may not be reproduced for use in a classroom or other group setting or for use by organizations as part of a training program. Such use may be granted by FranklinCovey in a written license and upon payment of applicable license fees; for information on becoming a licensed facilitator please call 1-800-272-6839.